More Praise for *Help Them Grow or Watch Them Go*

"Like eating your fruits and veggies, developing your employees should be done every day. Beverly Kaye and Julie Giulioni not only show how easy it can be but make the case that regular, short conversations can better develop people."
—**Charlene Li, founder, Altimeter Group, author of *Open Leadership*, and coauthor of *Groundswell***

"Life and business are all about where you pay attention. Pay attention to the growth of your people...and they will grow your business. The authors do a great job in spelling out the how-tos!"
—**Chip Conley, founder, Joie de Vivre Hotels, and author of *Emotional Equations***

"Developing talent is essential for business success. This book provides a practical and easy-to-implement approach that can have a big impact on an organization."
—**Tamar Elkeles, Chief Learning Officer, Qualcomm**

"One of the most important responsibilities of a leader is to grow future leaders. The authors do a great job making development something that can happen during one's everyday work life."
—**Gabriella Giglio, Executive Vice President for Global Human Resources, American Express**

"Should be the career conversation bible for busy leaders!"
—**Marshall Goldsmith, author of the *New York Times* bestsellers *Mojo* and *What Got You Here Won't Get You There***

"The authors provide pragmatic insights and tools for managers to make employee growth a *part of work versus apart from work* with their people in the midst of rapid, ongoing change. After reading this book, it will be impossible not to see what one can start doing immediately to be more effective."
—**Teresa Roche, Vice President and Chief Learning Officer, Agilent Technologies**

"*Help Them Grow or Watch Them Go* is an important contribution to leading organizations where people and talent growth matters to success."
—**Kevin Wilde, Vice President and Chief Learning Officer, General Mills**

"The best and most comprehensive resource available. It takes the complex issue of career development and simplifies it with real, action-oriented tips, tools, and insights. It's relevant for new supervisors, senior executives, and HR professionals at any level, in any industry."
—**Sharon Silverman, Vice President, Human Resources, Macy's**

"Beverly Kaye and Julie Winkle Giulioni provide a practical, personalized approach that promises to help managers seeking to create an environment that

supports all members of a diverse workforce and empowers them to achieve their career growth aspirations."
—**R. Roosevelt Thomas, Jr., author of** *World Class Diversity Management*

"At last, a hands-on book that's smart, practical, and honest. Everyone knows that people make all the difference; this book will teach you how to make a difference with your people."
—**Alan Webber, cofounder,** *Fast Company*, **and author of** *Rules of Thumb*

"Improving the skills of our workforce is one of the country's most important economic challenges. It has to start with employers, and *Help Them Grow* tells you how to do it painlessly."
—**Peter Cappelli, Director, Center for Human Resources, The Wharton School, and Professor of Management, University of Pennsylvania**

"Full of useful materials that are easy to access. Ideal for a manager who wants to learn about coaching others."
—**Edward E. Lawler III, Distinguished Professor of Business, Marshall School of Business, University of Southern California, and coauthor of** *Management Reset*

"Beverly and Julie have a remarkable gift of turning an important and complex topic into useful and simple ideas and practices. Their work will help leaders wisely invest in their employees and employees take responsibility for their personal development."
—**Dave Ulrich, Professor of Business Administration, Ross School of Business, University of Michigan**

"Provides a practical road map for managers who know that they want to help their teams but may not know the clear, specific steps they can take."
—**Rebecca Ray, Senior Vice President, Human Capital, The Conference Board**

"I loved this book. Draw from the abundant list of simple yet powerful questions and become the best talent manager in your organization."
—**Tina Sung, Vice President, Government Transformation and Agency Partnerships, Partnership for Public Service**

"Bev and Julie give us creative, fresh, and immediately applicable tools to spark career conversations in real time, in the moment—not once or twice per year. I've already applied a couple of suggestions from the book and received an immediate payback."
—**Lorraine Munoz, Director, Leadership Development, Boston Scientific Corporation**

"A great guidebook for those whose job it is to help other people grow, with all the right questions we need to be asking!"
—**Frances Hesselbein, President and CEO, The Frances Hesselbein Leadership Institute**

Help Them **Grow** or Watch Them **Go**

Help Them Grow or Watch Them Go

CAREER **CONVERSATIONS**
EMPLOYEES WANT

Beverly Kaye and Julie Winkle Giulioni

BK

Berrett–Koehler Publishers, Inc.
San Francisco
a BK Business book

Berrett-Koehler Publishers, Inc.
1333 Broadway, Suite 1000
Oakland, CA 94612-1921
Tel: (510) 817-2277 Fax: (510) 817-2278 www.bkconnection.com

Ordering Information

Quantity sales. Special discounts are available on quantity purchases by corporations, associations, and others. For details, contact the "Special Sales Department" at the Berrett-Koehler address above.

Individual sales. Berrett-Koehler publications are available through most bookstores. They can also be ordered directly from Berrett-Koehler: Tel: (800) 929-2929; Fax: (802) 864-7626; www.bkconnection.com.

Orders for college textbook/course adoption use. Please contact Berrett-Koehler: Tel: (800) 929-2929; Fax: (802) 864-7626.

Orders by U.S. trade bookstores and wholesalers. Please contact Ingram Publisher Services: Tel: (800) 509-4887; Fax: (800) 838-1149; E-mail: customer.service@ingrampublisherservices.com; or visit www.ingrampublisherservices.com/Ordering for details about electronic ordering.

Berrett-Koehler and the BK logo are registered trademarks of Berrett-Koehler Publishers, Inc.

Printed in the United States of America

Berrett-Koehler books are printed on long-lasting acid-free paper. When it is available, we choose paper that has been manufactured by environmentally responsible processes. These may include using trees grown in sustainable forests, incorporating recycled paper, minimizing chlorine in bleaching, or recycling the energy produced at the paper mill.

Library of Congress Cataloging-in-Publication Data
Kaye, Beverly L.
    Help them grow or watch them go : career conversations employees want / by Beverly Kaye and Julie Winkle Giulioni.
        p.   cm. -- (A BK business book)
    ISBN 978-1-60994-632-6 (pbk.)
    1. Career development.   I. Giulioni, Julie Winkle.   II. Title.
    HF5549.5.C35K39   2012
    658.3'124—dc23   2012022139

First Edition

19 18 17 16 | 15 14 13 12 11 10

Produced by BookMatters, text and cover designed by Nancy Austin, copyedited by Tanya Grove, proofed by Janet Reed Blake, indexed by Leonard Rosenbaum.

From Julie,

To Peter for knowing I could do this...and making sure I did.

To Nick and Jenna for the constant joy and lessons learned from watching you grow.

From Beverly,

To Barry for truly being the wind beneath my wings.

To Lindsey for showing me that I still have a lot to learn.

CONTENTS

INTRODUCTION

WHAT'S A MANAGER TO DO?

Developing employees. Helping them grow. It's like eating properly or exercising.

You know it's good. You know you should. Yet, if you're like many managers today, you just don't do it as well or as frequently as you would like.

In survey after survey, year after year, employees express their dissatisfaction with how they are being supported in their careers. At the same time, managers across industries, regions, and levels uniformly report a moderate to severe lack of competence, comfort, and confidence in themselves in regards to this critical job expectation.

What IF . . .

► you could more easily and frequently engage in the career development work that employees crave without sacrificing everything else that must get done?

► employees learned to assume greater responsibility for their careers?

► it was possible for career development to be integrated into the work that needs to get done as opposed to being a separate series of overwhelming tasks that have to be checked off a list?

. . . .

You could. They can. And it can be. That's why we've written this book.

HELP THEM gRO**W**

Career development is as important as it's ever been (maybe more). In today's business environment, talent is *the* major differentiator. And developing that talent is one of the most significant drivers of employee engagement, which in turn is the key to the business outcomes you seek: revenue, profitability, innovation, productivity, customer loyalty, quality, and cycle time reduction.

But the reality of career development is changing in response to the new business landscape. It's not the wide-open playing field it once was. Boomers are waiting longer to retire. Repeated rounds of belt tightening have led to delayering and downsizing. More jobs are outsourced. All of this breeds a sense of scarcity and leaves the impression that there aren't as many opportunities as there once were. This makes career development more—not less—important than in the past.

OR WATCH THEM *GO*

Ignore the development imperative at your own peril. Every day, employees who believe that their careers are not getting the attention they deserve make the decision to leave. Some resign to pursue employment in organizations that offer greater opportunity. Others decide the freelance life fits them better, and they cobble together a variety of projects that become a career.

But an equally dangerous situation occurs when employees stay but withdraw their engagement, motivation, and enthusiasm for the work.

CAREER CONVERSATIONS EMPLOYEES WANT

So, what's a manager to do? Plenty. And it might be easier than you expect. Quality career development boils down to quality conversations.

Throughout this book, we'll challenge you to reframe career development in such a way that responsibility rests squarely with the employee, and that your role is more about prompting, guiding, reflecting, exploring ideas, activating enthusiasm, and driving action. This role centers around talking about—rather than actually *doing* the heavy lifting of—development.

We'll offer a framework for thinking about conversations that help others grow. It involves three distinct types of conversations: hindsight, foresight, and insight.

▶ Hindsight conversations are those that help others look backward and inward to determine who they are, where they've been, what they love, and where they excel. Chapters 3 and 4 provide you with questions and ideas for helping others look back as a basis for moving forward.

▶ Foresight conversations are designed to keep employees looking forward and outward toward changes, trends, and the ever-evolving big picture. Chapter 5 offers easy, straightforward tools that are long on value and short on your time investment.

▶ Chapters 6, 7, and 8 focus on leveraging the insights that surface from the convergence of hindsight and foresight. How do the employees' strengths fit into where the organization or industry is going? Where are there opportunities to carve out space to grow and perform? Out of the work that needs to be done, which activities will give people unique experiences and fodder for development?

▶ In Chapter 9, you'll learn how to grow with the flow or embed development into everyday life through heightened awareness and fluid conversation strategies.

HOW TO READ THIS BOOK

You're probably doing a pretty good job so far. Here are just a few thoughts to get the most from the experience.

This book was written for anyone who has a role in developing others. The titles vary from organization to organization: Supervisor,

Manager, Director, Team Leader, Vice President, CEO. We've chosen to use the term *manager* generically. Whenever you see it, it means *you*.

This book is all about the career conversations employees want. So we'll draw heavily upon employees' voices. These are real individuals in the workplace whose eloquent insights make the point far better than we could. They aren't the entitled whiners with unrealistic expectations. They're your solid citizens. The ones you count on to produce. The ones you're hoping will stick around.

▶ TRY THIS

You'll find lots of questions and activities you can use with your employees. We'll call them out like this. Have an upcoming career conversation? Scan the pages for an exercise, tuck the book under your arm, and you're ready to go.

WHAT ABOUT YOU?

So, you're somebody's employee too, right? And, if you're like many managers, you get caught in the middle, doing the right thing for your employees, but not necessarily having it done for you. As you read this book, you may find yourself thinking, this sounds pretty good, but what about me? Answer: do it yourself!

The tools and questions throughout this book are highly flexible. Change **you** to I and you're ready for some self-discovery. You might find it helpful to review the answers with someone at work or at home. A fresh set of eyes may pick up clues and offer a different perspective and new insights.

We'll close each chapter with some *what if*s. We know that as a manager responsible for delivering business results, you must keep your feet planted firmly on the ground. So, from that grounded position, take a moment to consider what just might be possible.

What IF . . .

▶ you kept reading and tried out even one or two ideas with your employees?

. . . .

They would *grow*.

1

Develop
Me
OR I'm
History!

Spending 40-60-80 hours somewhere each week . . .

I want it to mean something. I want to feel like I'm moving forward somehow. If I can't grow here, I've gotta look elsewhere.

—an employee (perhaps yours)

The decision to assume a management role in today's workplace comes with a front-row seat to some of the greatest business challenges of our time. Day in and day out, you must

Do more with less. It's become cliché, but it permeates life at work. You've likely become a master at finding ways to reduce costs, time, and other resources below levels you never imagined were possible.

Meet ever-expanding expectations. Every quarter, you're asked to do a little (or a lot) more. Bigger sales. Greater numbers of service interactions. More projects. Higher scores.

Continuously improve quality. Good enough isn't. Given the competition in today's global market, perfection is the standard—until it's met and you have to do even better.

Deliver the next big thing. Most organizations believe that if they're not moving forward, they're sliding back. Innovation gets its picture on business magazine covers because it represents the promise of greater success.

And, no matter how long, hard, or smart you work, you can't do all of this alone. Success depends upon tapping the very best that each employee has to offer and enabling the highest possible levels of engagement.

Study after study confirms that best-in-class managers—the ones who consistently develop the most capable, flexible, and engaged teams able to drive exceptional business results—all share one quality: they make career development a priority.

Career development

is among the **most** frequently **forgotten tools** for driving business results...

yet

it's **completely within** a **manager's** sphere of **influence.**

A "HISTORY" LESSON

Even during challenging economic times, your best and brightest have options. Failing to help them grow can lead employees to take their talents elsewhere. They become "history." But what can be equally as damaging as this sort of talent drain are the employees who stay and become disengaged. Their bodies remain but their commitment has quit. In this way, history plays out, repeating itself over and over again in too many organizations.

So, if career development is a tool that can deliver productivity gains, expense reduction, quality improvements, innovation, and bottom-line results, why isn't everyone using it?

DEFINING TERMS

Perhaps it's frequently forgotten because the term *career development* strikes fear into managers' hearts.

> **WHAT ABOUT YOU?**
>
> Take a moment to think about what career development means to you? What's involved? What's your role?

Whatever your answer, we'll bet that ours is simpler. You see, many managers are intimidated by or steer clear of career development because they have a mistaken, convoluted, or overwhelming definition of the term.

So, try this definition on for size:

Career development
is nothing more than
helping others grow.
And nothing less.

Helping others grow can take a nearly unlimited number of forms. On one end of the continuum, you help employees prepare for and move to new or expanded roles in obvious and visible ways. But far more frequently, growth shows up on the other end of the continuum, in small, subtle ways that quietly create greater challenge, interest, and satisfaction in a job.

The problem is that too often career development evokes images of forms, checklists, and deadlines. And let's be honest—you've got to address them to support the organization. But administrative details are not career development.

Instead, genuine and meaningful career development occurs through the human act of conversation.

Whether it's a formal individual development planning (IDP) meeting or an on-the-fly connection, it's the quality of the conversation that matters most to employees. That's how they judge your performance and their development. That's also how they make the decision to go or stay—or to stay and disengage.

So, if it really is as simple as just talking to people, then why isn't career development a more common feature of the organizational landscape?

IMMOBILIZING MYTHS

Over the years, managers—by sharing oral history and spinning lore—have created and continue to propagate several myths. And these myths (read: reasons or excuses) keep them from having the very career conversations their employees want. Which are familiar to you?

Myth 1 — There is simply not enough time.

No one will argue that time is among the scarcest resources available to managers today. But let's get real. You're having conversations already—probably all day long. What if you could redirect some of that time and some of those conversations to focus on careers?

Myth 2 — If I don't talk about it, they may not think about it and the status quo will be safe.

Why invite problems? Developing people could lead them to leave and upset the balance of your well-running department, right? Wrong. Employees have growth on their minds—whether you address it or not. Withholding these conversations is a greater danger to the status quo than engaging in them.

Myth 3 — Since employees need to own their careers, it's not my job.

No one will argue that managers don't own the development of their employees' careers. Employees do. But that doesn't mean that managers are completely off the hook. You have an essential role in helping and supporting others to take responsibility. And that role plays out in large part through conversation.

Myth 4 — Everyone wants more, bigger, or better: promotions, raises, prestige, power.

If you believe this one, then your employees all look like baby birds, their mouths always wide open, wanting to be fed. This image probably loses its appeal quickly even for doting bird parents—much less busy managers. But based upon our research, this image is patently inaccurate. When asked about what they want to get out of a career conversation with their managers, the number-one response from employees is "ways to use my talents creatively."

Myth 5 — Development efforts are best concentrated on high potentials, many of whom already have plans in place.

This one's a cop-out. You can indeed see a significant return on the development you invest in your high potentials. But they make up only about 10 percent of your population. You probably have another 10 percent of marginal performers who are on a very different kind of plan. But what about the 80 percent in between—the massive middle responsible for doing the bulk of the work? Imagine what even a small investment in their development might yield.

Careers are developed one **conversation** at a **time...** over time.

If you're like most managers, a few of these myths likely make sense to you. Dog-ear or bookmark these pages and come back to them after you've completed the book. We predict that once you are introduced to a different way of looking at your role, you may also look at career development and these myths a little differently.

But, until then, remember this: growing the business means growing people. Forget that . . . and the rest is history.

What IF . . .

▶ you reframed how you think about career development?

▶ growth really was as simple as conversing with employees?

▶ managers could break through the myths that undermine their success and their employees' growth?

. . . .

2

Can We Talk?

I am realistic. I know your time is tight and that you've got lots of other priorities. My career probably isn't at the top of your list. Don't worry . . . I've gotten the message that I own my career. I just need a "thinking partner" who'll help me step back every once in a while and focus on my development.

—an employee (perhaps yours)

If you're like most managers, you care. You've become accustomed to taking on more and more, expanding your job description with countless "other duties as assigned"—and even some that aren't. Developing the careers of the people who report to you is on a growing (read: crushing) list of to-dos.

What if you could reimagine your role around helping others grow? What if you reframed this task (which, let's face it, gets put on the back burner most of the time anyway) in such a way that responsibility rests squarely with the employee? What if your role was more about prompting, guiding, reflecting, exploring ideas, activating enthusiasm, and driving action rather than actually doing all the work?

Guess what? That's how it should be. That's how you help people take responsibility for their careers. That's also how you can fit career development into your already full day.

Somehow the simple human act of helping people grow has gotten very complicated—processes on top of checklists with references to resource guides—and the to-do list keep growing. Is it any wonder that you want to steer clear?

But managers who do this well cut through the clutter and have figured out what employees really need. And it's much more basic than you might imagine.

> **"**I got tired of orchestrating these development experiences for
> people who just blew them off like they were nothing. I finally
> saw that the gift of 'heavy lifting' I was giving my people was
> not appreciated. If I owned their development plans, they didn't.
> So I backed way off. Now, I'm totally there for them, will talk it all
> out, explore possibilities, help them think it through. But, when it
> comes to making it happen, they've got to take the lead. That's
> their job.**"**

— Manager, Logistics

For years we've heard that "talk is cheap." Not true.

Astute managers have gotten comfortable with talking more and doing less. These are no slugs—they're strategists. They appreciate the power of conversations to inspire and generate change in others.

Conversation has the power to touch employees' hearts and minds more deeply than the well-intentioned steps a manager might take on their behalf. You need nothing more than your own words to spark reflection and commitment. From that can spring employee-generated actions. Actions that employees own. Actions that will help them realize their personal definitions of success.

Career development is all about the conversation.

> **"**The action is in the interaction.**"**

— Douglas Conant, former Campbell Soup CEO
and author of *Touchpoints*

Genuine career development is not about forms, choreographing new assignments, or orchestrating promotions. It's about the quality of the conversations between a manager and an employee, conversations that are designed to

► Facilitate insights and awareness

► Explore possibilities and opportunities

► Inspire responses that drive employee-owned action

When it comes to the **manager's role** in development, **talk** is **actually the most precious** and results-driving commodity you have to share.

NEW YEAR'S RESOLUTIONS

In some organizations, time is set aside each quarter, twice a year, or annually for managers and employees to engage in career dialogue. If you find yourself in that sort of environment, appreciate it. It's rare.

If you're like the vast majority of managers, you don't have the luxury of such sacred time. Because you operate at the speed of business, it's hard to imagine slowing down for a leisurely hour to discuss development.

So, here's the good news. You don't have to hold lengthy summits with employees, solving all of the career problems of the world in one big meeting to help others get results. In fact, in many cases less can be more.

" After a few years, I realized what the annual development process reminded me of . . . New Year's resolutions! It was energizing to set out the plan . . . and we paid attention to it for a while. But pretty soon, it was tucked away until the following year when we'd smile at our folly and rededicate ourselves to a new batch. "

— Marketing Director

When you reframe career development in terms of ongoing conversations—rather than procedural checkpoints or scheduled activities—suddenly you have more flexibility and the chance to develop careers organically, when and where authentic opportunities arise.

LESS IS MORE

An interaction doesn't have to have a minimum threshold to count as a conversation. You don't get more points for length. You get more points for stimulating thinking.

Would you rather . . .

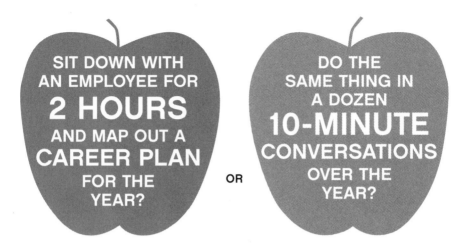

Note: Do the math. In this apples to apples comparison, it's the same 120 minutes just offered up in smaller, bite-size servings.

Increasingly, time-starved managers are opting for shorter, more frequent conversations that can cover the same ground as their heftier cousins (maybe more) but in an iterative and ongoing fashion. The benefits are compelling:

- Shorter conversations fit better with the cadence of business today.
- Frequent, ongoing dialogue communicates a genuine commitment to the employee and development.
- Iterative conversations allow employees to layer awareness, insights, and action more naturally.
- The ongoing nature of the conversation keeps development alive in everyone's mind (vs. tucking it away for a formal meeting).
- These frequent exchanges sustain momentum, fuel progress, and act as an ongoing reminder of the organization's commitment to employee learning, growth, and progress.

Some call it *embedded*. Others *catch-as-catch-can*. We call it a contemporary solution to a perennial problem. Short, targeted, ongoing career conversations are efficient—for you and the employee—because they happen within the workflow where genuine opportunities exist.

BECOME UNBALANCED

Think about the most interesting and engaging conversations you've experienced. Either you got to do most of the talking or the dialogue moved fluidly back and forth allowing everyone to share airtime evenly. Now, forget all that.

A career conversation is completely unbalanced in favor of your employees. If you do your job well, they will be doing 90 percent of the talking. If you're talking more than that, you're likely taking on too much responsibility for their development and robbing them of ownership for their careers.

Striking this unbalance requires a particular skill on the part of the manager: asking quality questions.

"My first real manager had this way of asking these questions that wormed their way into my brain and ultimately demanded answers."

— Supervisor, Finance and Accounting

If the work of career development happens within the context of conversation, then the primary tool of the trade must be the question.

Thoughtfully conceived and well-timed questions make things happen. They

► Provoke reflection, insight, constructive discomfort, ideas, and action in others

► Keep the focus squarely on the employee

► Demonstrate that you respect and value the other person

► Reinforce the shift of ownership for development to the employee

We are so sold on the value of questions, that we've included one hundred throughout this book.

You **don't**
have to have
all the
answers.

But,
what's **not negotiable**
is that you
have the
questions.

??????????

CULTIVATING CURIOSITY

Questions are a powerful tool. Add a spirit of curiosity, and you've got an unbeatable combination. People recognize and respond to genuine curiosity on the part of their leaders.

WHAT ABOUT YOU? ·

You might be able to fake listening, but not curiosity. Test your own Curiosity Quotient (CQ).

I am comfortable entering a conversation not knowing how it will turn out.	❏ YES	❏ NO
I can suspend judgment and skepticism.	❏ YES	❏ NO
I expect to be surprised when I talk with others.	❏ YES	❏ NO
I can suspend my need to fix situations and solve problems.	❏ YES	❏ NO
I am sincerely interested in what most people have to say.	❏ YES	❏ NO
I believe that there's no shame in admitting I don't understand something.	❏ YES	❏ NO
I ask questions without having a "right" answer in mind.	❏ YES	❏ NO
I am energized by finding out what makes others tick.	❏ YES	❏ NO
I am motivated to dig deeper when I sense hesitancy or want to learn more.	❏ YES	❏ NO
I enjoy learning things about people that I didn't know before.	❏ YES	❏ NO
I am comfortable following someone else's lead in a conversation.	❏ YES	❏ NO
I believe that people are interesting and complex.	❏ YES	❏ NO

If you answered no to four or more, then you have an opportunity to cultivate greater curiosity. But you're likely an overachiever and realize that even one no offers a chance for improvement.

Curiosity might be the most under-the-radar and undervalued leadership competency in business today. Think about it: what could you accomplish if you practiced passionate listening—really listening with intention and a true sense of purpose to learn and understand? What ideas and possibilities could you cultivate if you honed your ability to wonder out loud with those around you?

Developing the ability to approach individuals, situations, and conversations with curiosity and even a sense of wonder can affect your own energy and enthusiasm, relationships with others, and hard business results—not to mention the quality of your career conversations.

Quality questions asked *without* curiosity will signal to employees that you've just come back from training.

Quality questions asked *with* the spirit of curiosity will facilitate conversations that will literally allow others to change their lives.

CLOSURE IS OVERRATED

Given this focus on asking questions, it bears repeating that you don't have to have all the answers. Neither does the employee, for that matter. In fact, not having all the answers may actually drive more thought and energy.

According to Russian psychologist Bluma Zeigarnik (in "The Retention of Completed and Uncompleted Actions," which appeared in *Psychological Research* in 1927), we remember better what's incomplete. The problem is that this lack of closure generates an internal tension for many. The mind, uncomfortable with what has been left unfinished, continues to focus on the question or problem.

So, what does this science have to do with helping your people grow? Many managers shy away from hard questions and conversations where they might not have all the answers. If you're one of them, you don't have to do that any longer. Quite the opposite. Go ahead and courageously ask the challenging questions and even end the conversation with a real tough or thought-provoking one that the employee can contemplate for a while.

Don't feel the pressure to wrap up every conversation with a bow.

Closure is overrated.

Unfinished business . . .

that's what will cause employees to continue to ponder and will ultimately ✳**spark**✳ action and **feed progress.**

▶ TRY THIS: OPEN ENDED
· ·

End your next meeting or conversation with a question. Explain that there's no time for a discussion, but that you've been thinking about it. The next time you are with that person or those people, ask if anyone remembers the question. You'll be surprised that not only do they remember the question, they'll also have quite a few answers for you.

HINDSIGHT, FORESIGHT, INSIGHT

So, what are all these unbalanced, curious, unfinished conversations supposed to be about? More than you might expect. Too frequently we limit the scope of career conversations, thinking they're only about jobs, promotions, or stretch assignments—the actions employees can take to move forward. Important? Yes. But that's just a drop in the bucket of conversations you can have with employees.

Whether your conversations are more formal and lengthy or shorter and iterative, helping others pursue their career goals involves facilitating an exploration of three key areas: hindsight, foresight, and insight.

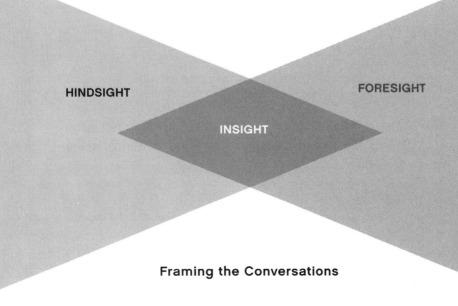

Framing the Conversations

Hindsight is a look backward to develop a deep understanding of such things as where employees have been, what they love, and what they're good at. Self-perception is key; and it becomes even clearer when enhanced (and sometimes moderated) by feedback from others. This backward glance—on the part of employees and those around them—is essential for moving forward.

Foresight involves a bigger-picture look at the broader environment and the business in order to determine what's changing and what those changes mean for the future. Since nobody wants to pursue a career direction for which no need exists, foresight is critical.

Insight is the sweet spot where hindsight (where you've been and what you want to be doing) converges with foresight (organizational needs and opportunities). It's where you jointly determine with employees the full range of ways to move forward and the actions to take to achieve career objectives.

This is not an academic model cooked up in a social science lab. It's a framework (based upon 30+ years of working with real people and their real challenges) that flexes to address the many types of career conversations available to managers. You'll find that it operates and supports you on three different levels.

Micro — You can ask a question from any of the three areas to informally spark reflection and interest.

Macro — You can blend the three areas into one short conversation that can occur spontaneously in the workflow to help employees advance their career thinking.

Mega — You can apply this framework and the questions associated with hindsight, foresight, and insight to your organization's formal individual development planning (IDP) process for richer results.

The following chapters delve into hindsight, foresight, and insight and how you can use them to keep employees satisfied, engaged, and always growing.

What IF . . .

▶ employees really owned their own careers?

▶ your job was to facilitate conversations rich with insightful questions that would guide others toward greater awareness and action?

▶ these conversations were shorter, more frequent, and occurred within the natural flow of the work?

▶ you didn't pressure yourself to have all the answers?

. . . .

3

Let
Hindsight
Light
THE Way

My interview for this job was so great. The manager was really interested in learning about my background and how I'd applied myself in the past. He asked great, probing questions that really challenged me to think. I sure wish he would "interview" me like that again now that I've got the job.

—an employee (perhaps yours)

Imagine if the job interview was the beginning of an ongoing conversational thread throughout someone's career. Imagine uncovering layer upon layer of your employees' skills, abilities, interests, and more—right up to the day they retire. Imagine what you could do with that information. Imagine what employees could do with it.

LOOKING BACK TO MOVE FORWARD

You can enable career-advancing self-awareness by helping employees take stock of where they've been, what they've done, and who they are. Looking backward thoughtfully is what hindsight conversations are all about. They surface what people need to know and understand about themselves to approach future career steps in a productive and satisfying way.

For hindsight to be as clear as possible, though, two different perspectives are required. Employees' self-perception is the starting point. (That's what this chapter is all about.) But it needs to be confirmed, challenged, enhanced, and otherwise worked over with information gathered from others. When employees, co-workers, and you (the manager) also look backward at performance and results, hindsight gets that much closer to 20/20. (Just wait until the next chapter for more about feedback.)

Hindsight allows employees to develop a clear view of their

► Skills and strengths—what they're good at

► Values—what's most important

► Interests—what keeps them engaged

► Dislikes—what they want to steer clear of

► Preferences—how they like to work

► Weaknesses—what they struggle with

Clarity around these factors allows for intentional movement toward career objectives. Otherwise, people may engage in lots of activity that's not focused or that takes them in directions that aren't consistent with who they are and what they really want to do.

> **"I worked for years to get that senior troubleshooter promotion. Put everything into it. But when I got it, I was miserable. The travel took me away from my family for weeks on end and the work itself was really unsatisfying. I'd swoop in, do my part, and then swoop out—never seeing the end product or really feeling a part of it. If I'd really thought about it, I would have known that it wasn't a good fit. I've always been happiest being part of an ongoing team and having something tangible to show for my efforts at the end of the day."**
>
> —IT Consultant

Hindsight conversations are the foundation of career development. They are designed to spark thinking, encourage connections, and promote discovery. They provide invaluable information to employees and to you, the manager. You can facilitate this type of self-awareness through quality questions that

► Haunt employees, popping out around every corner

► Percolate throughout the day—and maybe the night

► Worm their way around their minds, finding new areas to explore

Your employees' ability **to take satisfying** and productive **steps** toward **career goals** is **directly proportionate to** their

self-aware-ness.

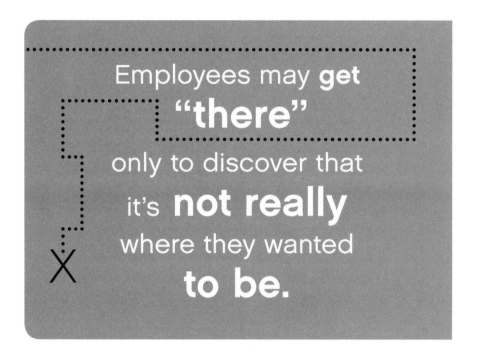

Employees may **get** "**there**" only to discover that it's **not really** where they wanted **to be.**

(If you're still waiting for the other shoe to drop and for us to tell you about the 10 to 20 hours of additional to-dos that are required to appropriately support your employees in their career development, let it go. It's not going to happen. We're serious. You can be highly effective by just guiding the conversation. You don't have to have the answers, and you don't have to drive the action. Really!)

THE GRAVITATIONAL PULL OF WEAKNESSES

Most people are disconnected from their strengths but strongly drawn toward their weaknesses. When you have a minute (literally 60 seconds), make a list of all of your strengths and weaknesses. Chances are you'll have more weaknesses than strengths on your list.

In fact, in workshop after workshop, we witness a surprising human dynamic. When people are asked to create a list of their weaknesses, they do so effortlessly, smiling and sometimes laughing at the task. Ask these same people to list their strengths and you see a very different response. Furrowed brows. Head scratching. Grimaces and genuine agitation. Odd, huh?

WHAT ABOUT YOU?

You can even skip the writing and count up your strengths on one hand and weaknesses on the other. More smiles or frowns?

So, employees need your help in identifying and focusing on what they do well—their talents and their gifts. These are important inputs to career decisions that frequently get lost in our weakness-centric world.

But strengths can be a little sneaky—and employees should be aware of two lesser-known laws that govern them.

Law 1 — Too much of a good thing isn't always a good thing. A strength used to excess can actually become a problem.

When it's just right	When it's overdone
"He's organized and meets deadlines no matter what."	"You mean old steamroller?"
"Her flexible thinking really helps everyone think outside the box."	"Our weekly meetings are a total waste of time because of her lack of structure."
"He's a great negotiator."	"It wouldn't hurt him to compromise once in a while."

Strengths have a dark side. Getting in touch with the implications of too-much-of-a-good-thing helps to enhance self-understanding—and ultimately effectiveness.

Law 2 — Strengths are context sensitive. A strength in one setting can actually work against you in other settings. (Remember when you were first promoted into leadership? Did your strength around getting the work done ever get in the way of delegating or developing others?)

A **strength** is a lot like **oxygen**.

We don't really pay much attention to it— unless it's missing.

But with all this talk of strengths, let's not lose sight of the importance of understanding weaknesses, where behavior or performance could compromise employees' career objectives or goals. Because when it comes to helping people grow and pursue career goals, a balanced view of what's working for and against you provides the strongest foundation for results.

Hindsight conversations don't need to be long or take a lot of planning time. Here are three approaches that you can prepare for in 2 minutes and conduct in as little as 5- to 10-minute chunks around the other work that needs to get done. Choose any or all depending upon your level of comfort and the nature of the relationship you have with your employees.

▶ TRY THIS: BACK TO THE FUTURE

Schedule a conversation to deliberately review an employee's past experiences, jobs, positions, and tasks to find themes, trends, and insights.

1. Start by explaining that a solid career future is based upon an understanding of who you are and what got you to where you are.

2. With the employee, create a list of the various positions, roles, and jobs she has held.

3. For each position, role, or job, ask the following questions:

    ▶ Which parts brought you joy, energy, and a sense of persistence?

    ▶ Which parts led to boredom, disengagement, and a sense of just going through the motions?

4. Step back with the employee and see what themes emerge. You won't need a PhD or psychoanalysis couch to start making the connections. Using questions like these will help:

    ▶ What thoughts/ideas repeated?

    ▶ How might your interests, values, and skills have evolved over time?

    ▶ What will you definitely want to seek out in the future?

    ▶ What will you definitely want to avoid in the future?

It's that straightforward. You ask the questions. They answer. And together you make sense out of it.

▶ TRY THIS: QUARTERLY CHECK-UP

A variation of the Back-to-the-Future theme is to close out every quarter with brief employee check-ups or check-ins. The purpose of these conversations is not to evaluate business results, review sales, or negotiate productivity standards for the next quarter. The goal is to diagnose what's going on in the employee's heart and head.

Put performance entirely aside and ask questions like these:

▶ What was the best part of the quarter for you?

▶ What work did you find most satisfying?

▶ How often were you stretched and how did that feel?

▶ At what points did you feel your energy and engagement lagging?

Make this a habit, and at least four times each year you'll help employees turn their day-to-day experiences into profound self-awareness that can inform career decisions—and a lot more.

▶ TRY THIS: THE NEVER-ENDING INTERVIEW
. . . .

Keep the interview going by engaging in routine conversations that reveal an ever-evolving, complex, and multidimensional picture to the employee of what will be important to consider as a basis for career growth.

1. Pull one or more questions that most interest you and the employee from the list that follows. Use them in any order. Take notes.

Skills and Strengths

▶ What have you always been naturally good at?

▶ What can't you keep yourself from doing?

▶ What are you known for?

Values

▶ Looking back, what's always been most important to you in life and in work?

▶ What issues or problems do you feel most strongly about?

▶ What are your top three values or things you hold most dear?

Interests

► What do you enjoy learning about most?

► What do you wish you had more time for?

► How would you spend your time if you didn't have to work?

Dislikes

► What kind of work have you typically gravitated away from?

► What tasks routinely get pushed to the bottom of your to-do list?

► What bores you?

Preferences

► What aspects of past jobs have you loved most?

► How do you like to work?

► What kinds of work settings/spaces help you do your best work?

Weaknesses/Opportunities

► What lessons do you find yourself learning over and over again?

► How do your strengths sometimes work against you?

► What skills do you appreciate in others that you don't always see in yourself?

2. Together determine what conclusions can be drawn by asking questions such as these:

► How do these pieces fall together?

► What picture/image does it yield?

► What are the commonalities, themes, or connection points?

Skills, strengths, values, interests, dislikes, preferences, and weaknesses converge in unique ways for each individual—like snowflakes or fingerprints.

As understanding about these things grows, people start to see an image appear that becomes a clearer and clearer picture of their lives and who they are.

But this awareness cannot be contained to just career matters. Greater personal insight can't help but spill over into day-to-day work, improving performance and results. Then it starts to seep out into one's personal life—enhancing that as well. Hindsight conversations are good for the whole person—not just for the part people bring to work.

Don't be fooled. These approaches are simple, straightforward, and relatively quick. But they pack a punch. In fact, they deliver value far beyond their modest appearances.

A CASE IN POINT

"I was born to teach. It was pretty obvious from the way I was frequently the first to figure out new processes and applications and teach them to the rest of the group. My earliest memory was of getting in trouble when I (proudly) taught a fellow kindergartner how to write the first letter of her name—on the carpet. Over the years, I've found my greatest satisfaction to be in roles where I connect with and help others learn and grow. I really appreciate my manager recognizing that and encouraging me to explore opportunities in training."

—Technical Trainer

COUNTERPOINT

"It's easy to pigeon-hole people. Figure out what they're good at and forget the rest. Take Pat, the rock star we hired away from a competitor to manage our challenging clients. Over the years, she seemed happy doing what she was doing. Once or twice we upgraded her title and raised her salary regularly. After all that, she resigned to take a sales job. It turns out that she had felt bored for years—was tired of what she was doing. If it had occurred to me to look past the one skill set that we myopically capitalized on, she'd still be with us today . . . and bringing in much needed new business."

—Director, Commercial Lines Insurance

Fundamentally people want to know themselves and be known by others. Hindsight conversations satisfy that deep human need.

But helping people look back and inward also provides a reservoir of information that allows employees to move forward and toward their career goals in intentional ways that will produce satisfying results.

What IF . . .

► a little time was spent looking backward before leaping forward?

► managers had the questions to help unlock what's unique within and important to each employee?

► you applied the curiosity you bring to first interviews to ongoing conversations with employees throughout their careers?

4

Feed Me

Where do I stand? How am I seen? What do *you* think? I don't mean to sound needy . . . but a little bit of information could go a long way with me.

—an employee (perhaps yours)

Feedback. How appropriate that the word begins with *feed*. Because for many employees, information from others about how they're perceived and how they're doing is currently a severe source of malnourishment in today's workplace.

Yet in study after study, employees in every sector are starving for feedback. And, it's a pretty human response. We spend 40+ hours each week at work, dedicating our bodies, minds, and souls to the cause. A little attention is not too much to ask.

Managers, beware. A low-feedback diet may be harmful to the health of your business. Side effects include

Disengagement Stunted growth
Lack of clarity Lost opportunities
Loss of talent

Good people move on—either psychologically or physically—when their hunger for feedback isn't satisfied. And this loss of talent is completely unnecessary because feedback

► Doesn't cost anything except a little genuine attention to others

► Lends itself to literally any setting—face-to-face or virtually—with no more than a moment's preparation

► Isn't just the domain of managers—anyone who is willing or asked can get involved

Feedback is a hindsight lens through which people can pass their self-perceptions—and in the process, it yields a clearer vision of who they are and the value they bring. Sounds good, right?

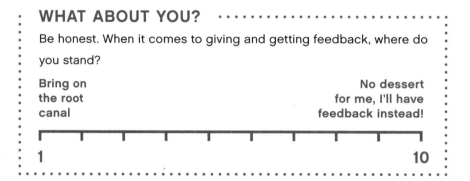

WHAT ABOUT YOU?

Be honest. When it comes to giving and getting feedback, where do you stand?

Bring on the root canal

No dessert for me, I'll have feedback instead!

1   10

IT'S FEEDING TIME

Opportunities for feedback abound. And what probably comes to your mind first is performance feedback—job-related information about an employee's behavior or results that helps to drive improvement. That's certainly important—but it's not what we're talking about here. We're talking about a broader and more expansive dialogue that drives development.

We've just discussed the value of hindsight conversations with employees, which surface essential information from their point of view. The problem is that an individual's perspective is rarely a complete picture. Employees need a reality check—an opportunity to expand their perspective beyond their own to round out their self-assessment. Voila! An opportunity for feedback.

When you help employees to proactively solicit the points of view of others, they get a twofer:

1. They're able to check their assumptions, balance their understanding of themselves, and discover who they are in the eyes of others.

2. They develop the capacity to independently initiate feedback conversations.

Do this well enough for long enough and pretty soon you'll have a self-generating feeding frenzy (in a good way) in which employees become comfortable getting and volunteering feedback freely among themselves.

WHO'S WHO IN THEIR ZOO

So feedback is another sort of a hindsight conversation. The good, the bad, and the ugly need to be confirmed or dispelled as employees' perspectives are checked against the points of view held by others.

To ensure the most complete picture, it's important to tap into the broadest career audience possible. Ask employees who might have additional insight into them, their strengths, abilities, interests, and opportunities.

The answer will likely include some combination of

Peers Employees Customers
Family Friends Manager

You'll notice that you are last on the list. And that's to make a point.

When it comes to **career** development, it takes
a **village**.

Employees need to develop the broadest network possible to facilitate their career success. Co-workers and others within and outside the organization have potentially important information, ideas, and helpful contacts. And gathering feedback from them is an ideal way for employees to begin to engage others in creating the path forward.

As a manager, you have a unique perspective. But yours is one of many that will inform employees' understanding of themselves and help to be the basis for effective planning.

Encourage employees to gather feedback from others before sharing your own. It's not about politeness (e.g., letting the guests get their food first) but about power. You've got it and, as a result, your perspective may carry undue weight. When employees come to you with a plate full of feedback from others, they are better able to put your perspective into perspective.

JUST REMEMBER: **ABC**

Soliciting and accepting feedback graciously are skills that distinguish successful and effective individuals. Yet, many people have not had the benefit of learning these skills. Your employees are likely among them.

Since the act of opening one's self up to the opinions of others can be challenging, the agenda for such a discussion should be simple—as straightforward as ABC. Encourage employees to focus on just three things as they gather feedback from others: abilities, blind spots, and conditions.

Abilities

► What are my greatest strengths?

► Which of my skills are most valuable?

► What can you always count on me for?

► What value do I bring?

Blind spots

► What behaviors have you observed that might get in my way?

► How have I fallen short of expectations?

► How might my strengths work against me?

► What one change could I make that would have the greatest positive effect on my success?

Conditions

▶ In what settings or under what circumstances do I make the greatest contributions?

▶ Under what conditions have you observed me struggling?

▶ Do I tend to perform best when working with others or flying solo?

▶ What factors have you noticed trigger stress or other negative reactions for me?

Work with employees to select a question or two from each category to use as the starting point for feedback conversations with individuals in their career networks.

As you can imagine, live, face-to-face feedback conversations are ideal. But, given today's distributed workforce, employees may need to resort to virtual means—phone or web-chat. Either way, this sort of real-time interaction can surface valuable information while strengthening relationships.

Greater awareness and stronger relationships support career development. In this way, feedback really does help employees grow where they are, so they won't go and grow somewhere else. As a bonus, they develop a critical skill that leads to greater success on the job and in life.

And, if you have an online tool that you love, keep using it—in addition to, not *instead* of, conversation.

HONEST ADVOCATE

You might have been at the end of that list of those who provide feedback, but you're not forgotten. You are a critical part of your employees' career audience too, which means that they'll be looking to you to share your perspective as well as your opinions about their abilities, blind spots, and the conditions that support their success. Your role is to be your employees' honest advocate, someone they can count on for support but also for candor.

Raw, real human

conversation

can be the most direct **path** to greater **awareness** and stronger **relationships**, even when it's unrehearsed and **clumsy**— perhaps **especially** when it's unrehearsed and clumsy!

❝I can hear almost anything she has to say because I know deep down that she's on my side.**❞**

—Registered Nurse

So that nurse and her boss are the exception, not the rule, right? You know how this works in your (read: real) life.

Only a subset of the universe of employees will seek out your feedback. Of those, only some will hear what you have to say. Some subset of that group will understand, and an even smaller number will then take action based on the feedback.

Given this reality, how can you justify putting effort into sharing feedback to help complement or complete employees' sense of self? You can't. You've got to do something to ensure that more people are hearing, understanding, and seriously considering your feedback. And this is something you can do.

▶ TRY THIS: FRAME YOUR FEEDBACK
· ·

A pair of practices will help deliver feedback so that employees can absorb it, understand it, and take action based upon it.

1. **Focus on the *what* and the *so what*.** The *what* refers to the specific, concrete behaviors and results that have a bearing on the employee's career direction and progression. Be as specific as you can be, sharing the details necessary to ensure a complete understanding.

   But, don't stop there. Address the *so what*. Explore the impact of the behavior and results you highlight. This provides a context for your feedback and helps the employee make sense of your feedback in terms of career development and direction.

   ▶ Don't say: You're a great rep. Keep up the good work.

   ▶ Do say: You consistently offer creative solutions to our customers' problems. Your behavior is the standard that new reps see and emulate. You're becoming a real leader of the team.

2. Use candor and care. This is not an either/or choice. It's both/and. The other person's ability to hear a tough message is directly proportionate to the care with which you deliver it. The few minutes you take to consider and frame your feedback can make a tremendous difference in terms of its reception and usefulness.

- ▶ Don't say: You just don't seem to be able to cut it in sales.

- ▶ Do say: You have the ability to develop strong relationships with customers. Those relationships, though, aren't translating into sales. Let's talk about where your strengths can be better used.

Recent brain researchers have found that people are more receptive to constructive (read: negative) feedback when it's preceded by a positive message. (Hmmm . . . you probably could have told them that.) Leading with strengths, talents, and skills lays the foundation and earns you the right to follow up with more sensitive information.

❝ Most people want to hear the truth, even if it is unpalatable—there is something within us that responds deeply to people who level with us. ❞

—Susan Scott, author of *Fierce Conversations*

A FEEDBACK FOCUS

Don't know where to start? Or do you want to expand your feedback focus to better support your employees' growth? Look no farther. Employees need to get information from you around three key areas: technical skills, soft skills, and a set of career intangibles.

Technical or *hard* skills are those that relate specifically to how employees produce the outputs of their jobs. Whether it's welding or website design, selling or shoemaking, it's the fundamentals of performing one's work—and what we typically think of first when we consider what's needed to be successful in a role.

But, that's just the tip of the iceberg. What's equally important (more important according to some) is the set of interpersonal or *soft* skills that enable someone's success. This includes communication, collaboration, teamwork, and networking. And anyone who's ever struggled to master them knows that these soft skills can be pretty hard.

There's yet another category of intangibles that are frequently forgotten. They operate below the surface as a set of often-unconscious competencies. Thirty years of field research has found that these qualities are key differentiators when it comes to day-to-day and long-term career success:

- ► Thirst for continuous learning

- ► Constant curiosity about the world and the possibilities it holds

- ► Sincere interest in continuing the journey toward self-awareness

- ► Resilience in the face of change

While people may be hardwired with a greater or lesser tendency toward these intangibles, they can definitely be developed over time—and with your supportive feedback.

Address any of these areas—technical skills, soft skills, or career intangibles—and you'll deepen self-awareness and plant important developmental seeds. Combine a couple for a powerful and enlightening conversation. Add them all to your list of possible feedback topics to address over time as you share your perspective in support of your employees' growth.

What IF . . .

- ► employees knew how to ask for feedback?

- ► managers were not the only ones providing it?

- ► all employees enjoyed clarity about who they are, what they're good at, where opportunities to improve exist, and where they could make the greatest difference?

5

What's

Happening

?

You don't have to tell me that the business landscape is changing. I know. I live it. But there's got to be a better way than always scrambling and reacting. I don't want to just keep up . . . I want to get ahead of the curve.

—an employee (perhaps yours)

We are not going to tell you the world is changing. You could write that book. The changes and challenges you face every day frame your decisions about strategy, resource allocation, and other critical business matters.

Shouldn't they frame career decisions as well? (Answer: A resounding yes.)

Hindsight conversations provide a solid grounding in who employees really are and what they bring to the party. But pursuing career growth with this clarity alone is a very dangerous thing. It can send people in directions that are interesting and may play to their strengths—but they might not serve a business need. (Read: dead ends.)

Hindsight clarity needs to be filtered through the lens of foresight. Foresight conversations open people's minds to the broader world, the future, organizational issues, changes, and the implications of all of these. Foresight helps others focus their career efforts in ways that will lead to satisfying and productive outcomes. (It also delivers the benefit of context and perspective that enhances day-to-day work. Another twofer.)

BEYOND THE CRYSTAL BALL

We've all heard stories about individuals who allowed their skills to become rusty and themselves to become antiquated. But what about those who anticipated the future and were ready to grow into it? These

Some people have an innate **ability** to keep their **eyes open** to the world around them.

To **spot trends** where others see u·n·c·o·n·n·e·c·t·e·d d·o·t·s.

To play out the implications of a **seemingly** insignificant event.

are the high-profile examples of business legends. But there are also the mere mortals who work on the ground floor and seem to have the gift of living just a little farther out in the future than the rest of us.

These people are probably not psychics. But they do practice their own brand of ESP: **E**ver **S**canning and **P**ondering.

While it may come naturally to some, you can nurture it in others. ESP is a set of habits—habits that you can help employees build through ongoing foresight conversations.

FOSTERING FORESIGHT

You've been to the meetings (or not) and read the memos (or not). You know the "big picture" for your organization (or not). You may lay awake at night worrying about it or you've so internalized it that it's always operating under the surface, unconsciously informing much of what you do. But your employees may have a more limited outlook.

So, populate their radar screens with a constellation of new points to consider:

▶ External challenges and changes—what's going on in the world— including changing demographics, globalization, government regulation, and economic instability

▶ Internal challenges and changes—what's going on within the organization—including changing customer expectations, new vendor relationships, mergers and acquisitions, and responses to shrinking margins

" Don't seat me at the kids' table. I might not be an executive, but I know there are changes coming. Let me in on things. I deserve to know, whether I can do anything about it or not." **"**

—Production Worker

Don't worry—we're not suggesting that you deliver a whole strategic planning curriculum to your staff. On the contrary, we're just suggesting that you create a forum for employees to get in touch with the world around them—the world that defines their career development playing fields.

▶ TRY THIS: HARNESS MORE HEADS

Whereas most career conversations are personal, one-on-one interactions between the employee and manager, foresight conversations are best enjoyed by a group. (And you'll enjoy the efficiency of this approach.)

It actually works best to get your team gathering information, researching issues, and having direct experiences that deliver a visceral understanding of business changes and challenges. In this case, two, three, four, or more heads are better than one.

Nobody can be an expert on all of the forces and factors shaping the world, business, or your organization—not even you. So, let the wisdom of your crowd take over. Encourage the activities and conversations that will help all employees develop the ESP habit.

Here's a starter list of ways people can begin to develop a visceral understanding of what's happening in the world around them. But between you and your employees, you'll likely come up with plenty more.

▶ Interview key individuals

▶ Engage in focused customer contact

▶ Research important issues or trends

▶ Read trade publications

▶ Participate in industry conferences

▶ Attend management or other cross-functional meetings

These activities will spark awareness and insight about the bigger picture, what's going on in the world, industry, and organization. But it's the conversation and reflection that follows that translates insight into a deep and useful understanding of the issues and their implications.

Encouraging
employees to
interact DIRECTLY
with the environment is just an
interesting exercise until
you **debrief** their experiences and
encourage **reflection**.

Simple questions that help people connect the dots go a long way:

► What are some of the most important things you learned?

► What might these things mean to our industry?

► What might they mean to our organization?

► How might they affect our products/services/revenue stream?

► How might they impact our department?

► What do they mean for you, your job, your career goals?

Individual **puzzle** **pieces** don't look like much. Put them **together** and you've got the **complete** picture.

FORESIGHT FORUMS

If you did this even occasionally, it would help, and you'd be doing more than most. Really want to make a difference? Consider institutionalizing foresight conversations by putting them on every meeting agenda. Have employees report on what they've learned. Hold open discussions using the questions listed above.

"I started asking different staff members to kick off our meetings with a brief headline review—something from a trade publication, business journal, or general news. They gave a two-minute overview of the article and led a brief discussion about what it meant to us. I was surprised by the insights the group generated and how engaged they became. One week I forgot to include it on the agenda—and they let me know about it.**"**

—Risk Manager

Imagine what could happen if you started each staff meeting with a focus on foresight. The results would be powerful. Every employee would develop greater clarity that would help to inform career decisions.

But you'll soon discover that this is only part of the benefits of group foresight conversations. *You* will learn more than you might expect. Employees will begin acting like business partners. You may even see more innovation and better results. Who knows what you'll accomplish . . . world peace? (That last one was just to make sure you were paying attention.)

► TRY THIS: FILL IN THE BLANKS
. . . .

Another approach to engaging employees in big picture conversations is just to set aside a few minutes and ask them to complete provocative sentence stems, such as

- ► The most significant change I've seen in our industry is _____
- ► I predict that the next big thing will be _____
- ► I can imagine a time when _____
- ► Our business would be turned upside down if _____
- ► Everything will change with the obsolescence of _____
- ► I was most personally affected when the organization changed _____

▶ It really made a difference when management _____

▶ To keep my edge and pursue my career goals, I'm going to need to

_____

Pick one or more. Do it individually. Or do it with the team as a whole. And watch the conversation unfold.

Don't be fooled. These sentence stems are as powerful as they are simple. They force employees—sometimes for the first time—to step back and think more broadly and strategically about the world around them and what it means for their careers.

WHAT ABOUT YOU?

Consider these sentence stems yourself. How would you complete them? What do your responses mean in terms of what you'd like to be doing with your career?

So hindsight is powerful but incomplete without the overlay of foresight. What's happening in the changing world around us plays directly into career decisions, strategies, and success. Employees can make these changes work for them with the help of some new habits— habits built and instilled through foresight conversations.

The intersection between hindsight and foresight is insight. And the possible insights are endless:

▶ A new skill might be deployed to solve a problem.

▶ Evolving interests might support a new business direction.

▶ A long-held goal might be pursued through a vital project.

Insights that are recognized, explored, and exploited through career conversations could uncover countless possibilities that will help employees and the business grow.

What IF . . .

► employees could develop the habit of scanning and pondering the environment around them?

► foresight conversations were a part of day-to-day life in your organization?

► everyone knew what was happening and what it meant for them?

6

If Not

UP...

Then What?

Challenge me. Stretch me. I'm not as worried about being promoted as I am about learning, growing, and seeing my talents used in new and different ways.

—an employee (perhaps yours)

Insight and growth are all about possibilities. But the problem is that managers and employees alike frequently have an outdated view of what those possibilities are. Growth in today's business environment means bidding adieu to some old thinking.

Say good-bye to the career ladder. The organizational belt-tightening and delayering that have occurred over the past several years have left far fewer leadership positions. The upper layers of the pyramid (which have always been slimmer) have become a mere sliver.

Say good-bye to limiting career paths. The predictable progression from one established position to the next has given way to career patterns. These are more fluid, flexible, and responsive to the needs of the business and the individual.

Say good-bye to checking your personal life at the door. We've moved beyond work/life balance to work/life integration. The convergence of technology and communication has blurred the lines for many between work and home.

A growing number of workers have come to the realization that they can't have it all—or at least not all at one time—and are not willing to sacrifice important parts of their lives for a job. Increasingly, people are deciding that work has to work for them.

Say hello to a new way of thinking about how careers happen—through a series of moves around, down, up, and over.

Today's career development looks more like a rock-climbing wall than a ladder.

Climbing Wall Wisdom 1 — The top doesn't have to be the goal. Frequently getting across or to a specific spot is exactly what you're looking to achieve.

"I'm happy at my current level. I don't ever want the headaches of being the boss. But I also don't want to stagnate where I am. I need to keep figuring out the next challenge, the next place I can make things happen."

— Technician

Climbing Wall Wisdom 2 — There are countless ways to get from point A to point B.

"I've reinvented myself several times over my career. Moving from sales to operations and now to customer service sure wasn't the straightest path, but I picked up exactly what I needed along the way."

— Customer Service Supervisor

Climbing Wall Wisdom 3 — Sometimes getting to your ultimate destination requires a move down the wall a bit.

"I really wanted to work in product development but knew I'd never be successful (or even considered) because I hadn't spent time in the trenches with the customer. So, I consciously downgraded my job title to get the experience that I needed. And, it all paid off in the end."

— Product Manager

Climbing Wall Wisdom 4 — You can choose safer or riskier moves, more or less secure foot-/handholds, depending upon the conditions that present themselves.

"When my youngest child became ill, I knew I couldn't keep up with the demands of my business development group. I had to make a decision. I'm grateful that my manager was open to helping me find another position with more regular hours. Now that everything is settled at home again, I'm happy to be back to my previous frenetic pace."

— Director, Business Development

The career-climbing wall is expansive, offering a **wide** selection of spots to **explore** and **enjoy**, and a nearly unlimited combination of **moves** in **every direction**— down ► around, up, over, and down —toward one's vision of **career success.**

ADVANCING THE NOTION OF ADVANCEMENT

The climbing-wall metaphor only works if we shift our mindset about what career progression and advancement really mean in today's environment.

You've been brainwashed into thinking that advancement means moving up in the organization: taking on more responsibility, managing larger staffs, and earning more money.

Advancement today means moving forward and toward a very personal definition of career success.

Do you know

▶ how your employees define career success?

▶ what kind of work they want to be doing?

▶ what they want to achieve?

▶ what talents they yearn to leverage or activate?

WHAT ABOUT YOU?

Ask yourself the same questions:

▶ How do you define career success for yourself?

▶ What kind of work do you want to being doing?

▶ What do you want to achieve?

▶ What talents do you yearn to leverage or activate?

You're in good company if you struggled with your own answers. You're in even better company if you don't know how your employees would answer. So, is it any wonder that career development is challenging? Most managers are flying blind.

Employees need to come to terms with what advancement means to them—how they personally define career success. And they need to let you in on that secret if they want your help and support.

As a result, some of the most important conversations you'll have with employees involve clarifying their definition of career success. A profound and thoughtful dialogue can be sparked by asking simple questions, such as

▶ Where do you see yourself in 2, 5, 10 years?

▶ What do you want to be doing?

▶ How do you want to be doing it?

▶ With whom and under what circumstances?

There simply is no cookie cutter approach for the customized, per-sonalized, tailored, just-for-me plan that advances each employee's unique career goals.

This is the part where you're thinking, "I knew that eventually it would get around to all the work that I have to do to manage my employees' careers." Right? Wrong.

Let's be clear. It's your job to facilitate the conversations that inspire insights, awareness, and action on the part of employees. You take the lead in the talk—asking, guiding, reflecting, exploring. They continue to own the action.

UP, DOWN, AND ALL AROUND

Understanding employees' definitions of career success is the first step. Pursuing those definitions can happen through any number of moves in a variety of different directions. Getting there may mean:

► Promotions to higher positions

► Lateral adjustments

► Steps that gain valuable experience that in the past might have been considered down or backward

► Even growing in place (Adapted from CareerPower, Career Systems International, ©2011.)

Up is what immediately comes to most people's minds when they think about career advancement. And, although there may be fewer opportunities closer to the top, vertical moves remain important and necessary. Organizations thrive when they have a pipeline filled with skilled internal candidates prepared to take on the challenges of the next level.

But, up is not the only way to go for employees looking for growth. In fact, in these days of flatter organizations, a lateral move is often the new promotion.

Sideways is not a consolation prize.

Quite the opposite. Increasingly, becoming knowledgeable about more of the organization is an asset.

Taking on a role at a similar level on the org chart broadens perspective. It encourages a more holistic view of the business. It activates a new and expanded network. And it builds agility, which is king in today's economy.

Recalibration is another option, although it won't win popularity contests with employees. How can you help others understand that moving from one level to another that may be considered lower organizationally is valid, honorable, and frequently strategic? (Answer: Begin by believing it yourself.)

Managers have to help employees see that it's **not**

down shifting.

It's just changing lanes, sometimes avoiding the traffic, and seeing new scenery in the process.

Sometimes the smartest move—and the fastest way forward—is to intentionally step back.

"I saw the writing on the wall. My division had a first class ticket to outsourcing. I wanted to stay with the company—and looked forward to leading bigger projects eventually. So, I moved over to another division. I went from managing three people to being an individual contributor again. I have to be honest . . . my ego took a hit for a while. But, I established myself quickly and learned a lot about a whole new group of customers. It was exactly what I needed to get me where I am today."

— Engineer

It can be a hard sell . . . but recalibration is frequently the best way for employees to progress forward toward their goals.

There's also the option of growing in place. But you'll have to stick around for one more chapter to learn about that.

So, clearly up is not the only way. And even if up is the preferred destination, the climbing wall—that is the business environment in which we all operate—offers lots of ways to get there.

What IF . . .

► employees viewed career progression more like a rock-climbing wall than a ladder?

► they pursued their career goals through a nearly unlimited combination of moves—over, around, up, and down?

► you talked to every single employee about what advancement and career success meant to them?

7

Same
Seat,
New
View

My friend worked for the same boss in the same department for nearly seven years. Sounds mind numbing, right? For him, it was anything but. His manager encouraged him to keep changing it up . . . helped him develop and really use his talents in all sorts of new ways. He grew way more than I did . . . even changing jobs every couple of years. That's the kind of manager I want.

—an employee (perhaps yours)

Be honest. All that talk of insight, possibilities, recalibration, and upward and lateral moves in the last chapter made you a little nervous, didn't it? As much as you'd like to help your employees transition into new roles that will support their growth goals, it's not always possible.

And that's why too many managers avoid career discussions altogether. You don't want to set unrealistic expectations only to disappoint when desirable moves are few and far between.

THINK GLOBAL, ACT LOCAL

Hindsight and foresight overlap to reveal insights into a whole world of development possibilities that exist for employees. Some involve moves, but (and here's the best-kept secret that will liberate development-minded managers everywhere) the vast majority do not.

Growth isn't limited to movements over, up, or down. With the right support, people can grow right where they're planted.

Growth in place is the most accessible yet most underutilized career development strategy available to managers. Let's face it. You may have little influence over getting an employee transferred or promoted, but you are completely in charge of what goes on in your own backyard. Finding ways to grow talents, explore interests, and build capacity within the context of employees' current jobs is completely within your sphere of influence.

Do you want to

▶ Raise engagement levels?

▶ Uncover and activate previously unknown or underutilized talents that can help the business?

▶ Establish a culture of continuous learning and development?

▶ Build the skills and knowledge needed so employees will be prepared when broader moves become available?

▶ Generate loyalty and the kind of leadership reputation that will have the best talent standing in line to work for you?

Help employees move forward and toward their career goals without making a move. Help them grow in place. Making this happen requires a shift in mindset.

TANGLED IN TITLES

The old mindset of career development involved a series of moves from position to position, title to title, toward one's dream job in a particular sequence:

If I want to be _____
                        (ultimate career goal/position)

then *first* I have to be_____
                        (lower-level title)

In the past, the classic career pattern involved bopping from role to role on the road toward that dream job. But we know that given today's reality, there just may not be that many positions or titles available. Does it mean that people who remain in the same role are condemned to pickling their minds, extinguishing their spirits, and not developing? (Answer: Absolutely not.)

The new model looks more like this:

If I want to be _____
(ultimate career goal/position)

then I have to know/be able to _____
(required skills)

" I figured out a long time ago that the job title doesn't mean nearly as much as the richness of the experiences it offers. Titles belong on books . . . not on people anyway."

—Retail Supervisor

Let's face it: even if it were feasible given today's leaner organizations, developing employees by continually moving them from position to position is exhausting. Development in place acknowledges the reality of the current workplace while meeting the needs of the employee and the organization.

The **challenge** of
growing in place
involves stripping titles
from our thinking and instead
focusing on what the employee
needs to experience, know,
learn, and be able to do.

When you **reframe** development in terms of identifying and sourcing necessary **experiences**, you **widen** the lens of **possibilities** and allow your people to grow right where they are.

Call it kismet—or just the product of quality career conversations—but a good manager can nearly always uncover ways to allow employees' interests and goals to find a home supporting the organization's needs. Good managers just seem to see opportunities where others do not.

"It was a head scratcher at first. My technical documentation specialist announced that she wanted to become a non-profit grant writer. We didn't have a lot of need for that in our for-profit manufacturing plant. But after thinking about it together, we realized that there were several skill areas shared by both roles. We figured out a way for her to develop her writing skills to improve the quality of her current projects and prepare her for creating grants. And she spent some time in sales helping to write proposals and other influence pieces. As a result, her engagement and commitment grew . . . and now she does some volunteer grant writing on the side."

— Documentation Manager

Managers who successfully support others growing in place are opportunity minded. Are you?

OPPORTUNITY MINDED OR BLINDED ·

Do you

See people as interesting, complex, and multi-dimensional?	❐ YES	❐ NO
Pick up on cues that employees are ready for something more?	❐ YES	❐ NO
Spot strengths that can be used in different or unusual ways?	❐ YES	❐ NO
See multiple ways of getting work done?	❐ YES	❐ NO
Squeeze learning from nearly every experience and interaction?	❐ YES	❐ NO
Cringe when you hear someone say, "But that's not how we do it around here?"	❐ YES	❐ NO
View job descriptions as helpful guidelines rather than handcuffs?	❐ YES	❐ NO
Initiate and engage in an ongoing conversation about how to maximize talent?	❐ YES	❐ NO
Feel energized by thinking outside of the box?	❐ YES	❐ NO
Resist seeing the world in terms of round pegs and square holes?	❐ YES	❐ NO

Analysis:

► If you answered yes 8 or more times, you are an opportunity visionary with 20/20 vision when it comes to finding ways to help employees seek out the circumstances they need to gain important skills, knowledge, and experiences.

► If you answered yes 5–7 times, you are opportunity minded and frequently see ways to connect your employees' career advancement needs with opportunities within the organization.

▶ If you answered yes 4 or fewer times, you may find that you are turning a blind eye toward opportunities to help your employees advance.

See *Love 'Em or Lose 'Em: Getting Good People to Stay* (Berrett-Koehler 2008) for more on opportunity mindedness.

Depending upon the dictionary, *opportunity* is defined as a set of circumstances that makes it possible to do something—in this case move forward and toward a personal definition of career success.

> Opportunity-minded managers **envision** and **enable** possibility-advancing **circumstances** with **employees**—through **conversation**.

This possibility generating is not haphazard. There is a method—and clear structure—to the madness of opportunity-minded managers. They understand that helping employees realize their definitions of career success requires conversations that fall into two distinct categories:

1. **WHAT** — Conversations that focus on *what* the employee needs in terms of experiences, skills, exposure, and information

2. **HOW** — Conversations that build on WHAT conversations and help the employee figure out *how* to get those needs met

CAUTION: To build opportunity mindedness in yourself and others, do not confuse these two conversations. Do not be tempted to combine them. And never reverse the sequence. Severe confusion and hair loss (because you'll be pulling yours out) will ensue.

One of the most common mistakes managers make is to jump directly from employees' career goals and definitions of success to "Here's what we're gonna do." And it's natural. As a manager, you didn't get to where you are by *not* being action oriented.

Moving prematurely to action causes you to shoehorn the possible into the practical far too early. It also

► Sidesteps important thinking

► Chokes off creativity

► Jumps to solutions before you know what the opportunity is

► Narrows the conversation

► Blinds you to the full range of possibilities

► TRY THIS: FIRST THINGS FIRST

Agree with the employee that you'll both suspend all talk of *how* to achieve what's needed. Instead focus jointly on determining WHAT is required for helping your employee move forward. Questions like these open up the possibilities:

► To reach your goal, what skills and knowledge will you need?

► What kinds of experiences will prepare you to be successful?

► What might you need more of?

► What might you need less of?

What you're looking for during this conversation are these kinds of responses:

▶ I need to broaden my business exposure.

▶ I've got to get more experience in different situations.

▶ I'd really benefit from getting closer to the customer.

▶ Developing a global perspective—that's what I need.

▶ I need to get some P&L responsibility under my belt.

▶ Can you help me create a strong support network?

▶ I'll have to increase the complexity of the leadership challenges I face.

What you're *not* looking for are these kinds of responses:

▶ I have to manage the customer care department.

▶ You've got to transfer me to John's group.

▶ I really need an administrative assistant.

▶ Please enroll me in the next management training series.

▶ I'd like your job, thanks for asking.

These sorts of responses are signals that the employee is skipping ahead to the HOW. Now, you understand the caution.

The objective of the WHAT conversation is to generate a broad pool of skills, experiences, information, and exposure that will support employees' advancement forward and toward their definitions of success. And opportunity-minded managers know how to make this happen.

IN A WORD

The opportunity minded share a whole language that shines the light on the nearly unlimited ways people can grow in place. Don't know the language? Use this development dictionary.

THE DEVELOPMENT DICTIONARY

Reconsider Experiment Raise

Learn Sharpen Specialize

Deepen

Expand Spread Extend Reinforce

Communicate Observe

Research

Challenge Broaden

Minimize Add Decrease

Seek Strengthen Return

Share Multiply Revive

Observe Intensify

Cultivate Test Look

Increase Practice Reenergize

Enhance Refresh

Those are powerful words. They are synonymous with growth. They get people thinking. They point employees in new and sometimes invisible directions. They establish or maintain momentum forward and toward employees' career goals. And this list is just the beginning!

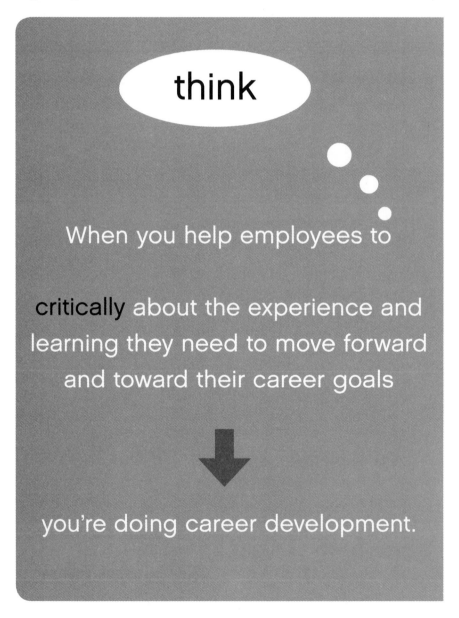

► TRY THIS: OPPORTUNITY WORD SEARCH

1. Share the Development Dictionary with employees to spark thinking about the experiences, skills, exposure, and information required to realize their career goals.

2. Ask them to pick as many words as apply and to use them as starters for phrases that describe what they need. (Example: "I need to broaden my network of resources" or "I need to sharpen my negotiating skills.")

3. Based upon your understanding of your employees' career goals, have a few ideas in your hip pocket to offer as well.

4. Discuss each to clarify and identify additional needs.

WHAT ABOUT YOU?

Which words appeal to you? What ideas do they prompt around what you need or want to develop your own career?

Pretty soon you and your employees will be fluent in the language of developing in place. You'll become opportunity minded because you open yourselves to the countless ways people can see a brand new view without ever having to make a move.

What IF . . .

► employees didn't think of their careers in terms of a litany of roles and titles?

► managers made the most of what they control: opportunities to grow within the division, department, or role?

► everyone became even just a little more opportunity minded?

► developing in place became as attractive as other options?

8

Advancing Action

We go through the exercise every year. Spend a bunch of time figuring out *what* I need to develop my career. Time's typically up just about when we get around to *how* to make it happen. I honestly think this does more harm than good. It's like a tease that gives me a hint of what's possible then slams the door on it—until next year when we do it all over again.

—an employee (perhaps yours)

Now to HOW. Remember the caution in the last chapter? Don't start working on *how* to make development priorities happen until after you've clearly identified *what* they are. Well, here is a second—and equally important—caution on the subject: don't forget to address the HOW altogether.

The work you do with employees around hindsight and foresight helps to generate insight into the world of possibilities that exist for those who want to move forward and toward their career goals. Identifying those possibilities is exciting and energizing. But those possibilities remain amorphous and abstract until they translate to action.

This translation doesn't happen magically or by chance. Rather, it happens through intentional effort—and intentional conversation between you and your employees.

Whether your employees wish to refresh their knowledge of a technical system, practice new work processes, sharpen their ability to identify the best deals, extend knowledge of one product line to another, strengthen interpersonal skills, or explore any other development priority that might be identified, you have three basic ways to make it happen. They are summarized in the 3E Model that follows. We've further adapted Cisco's adaptation of *The Career Architect Development Planner* by Michael M. Lomardo and Robert W. Eichenger (3rd edition, Minneapolis, MN: Lominger Limited, 2000).

The **3E** Model

▶ Expand **education** to being open to a variety of learning avenues.

▶ Enable **exposure** to others who can teach, mentor, and coach.

▶ Explore **experience** that will unlock opportunities to learn on the spot.

Understanding and using the 3Es will allow you to work with employees to actually move from insights to implementation.

BACK TO SCHOOL

When people think of learning and development, they naturally think of education. For the majority of us, school is where we got most of our instruction and did most of our growing up.

In the workplace, education takes many forms—both old- and new-school in nature. There are workshops on nearly any topic you can imagine. Community colleges offer credit and non-credit courses to build necessary knowledge and skills. In fact, MIT provides its entire catalog of online courses free of charge.

Learning isn't limited to live group settings though. For instance, E-learning allows for independent development whenever and wherever employees need it. TED talks and other informative videos are available 24/7 for just-in-time, just-for-me learning.

Webinars and virtual classrooms provide instruction while connecting people across the country or around the world.

▶ TRY THIS: SET UP FOR EDUCATION

It's easy to assume that if you've pointed employees in the right direction—or even signed them up for a class—then your role is over. After all, it's up to them. Right? Wrong. People get the most value from education when their managers help set them up for success. You'll see the best results if you follow these steps.

1. Set expectations in advance. Through conversation, you can support employees to powerfully focus their effort and learning. Intentional learning is stimulated by good questions.

   ▶ How will this learning help move you forward and toward your career goals?

   ▶ What specifically do you hope to gain?

   ▶ How will you use what you've learned?

   ▶ What challenges or obstacles might come up while you're learning?

   ▶ How will you address these challenges or obstacles?

   ▶ What are you willing to invest to make the most of this learning opportunity?

   ▶ What do you need from me? (This one's optional, but only because many managers are afraid this will lead to a lengthy list of to-dos. Just try it. You'll be amazed at the small requests that can lead to disproportionately large returns on learning.)

2. Set aside time. Scheduling employees into classes is easy. Preserving that time so they can focus on the learning at hand—that's tougher. Nothing says "Your education and development *don't* matter" any louder than pulling people out of seminars, interrupting webinars, or letting other priorities preempt learning commitments. In fact, one of the biggest employee complaints is the discrepancy between what managers say about their commitment to learning and their behavior. So, treat education like the real work that it is.

3. Set up opportunities to use what's learned. New skills and knowledge must be exercised to grow strong. Work with employees before, during, and after their educational experiences to find meaty and meaningful ways to apply, extend, and strengthen their learning.

4. Set a date to debrief. (More on this later.)

"Training used to be the panacea for everything. But with budget cuts and production pressures, managers are being more thoughtful about how to get the biggest bang from their employees' investment of time and money in training. They're getting more involved on the front end and the back end. And I think it's really paying off."

— Training Director

EXPOSE WISDOM IN THE WORKPLACE

By now, you've probably learned the refrain of this book by heart: you don't have to do it all. Facilitate exposure by facilitating connections. The more individuals who are drawn into an employee's career support circle, the better.

"Once I realized that—even if I had all the time in the world—I couldn't be all things to all people, it took a lot of pressure off. There are so many other people in the organization who are much better suited to help my folks learn what they need to know."

— Sales Manager

Enabling exposure through mentoring and networking costs virtually nothing. It can efficiently deliver learning, as well as many more organizational outcomes. The key is to help employees determine who are the best resources available. Start the dialogue with questions such as

► Who is known for . . . ?

► Which groups or teams have experience with . . . ?

► Who might know someone who can help you learn more about . . . ?

AN UPDATED VIEW OF EXPOSURE

When employees are looking to learn and grow, they frequently focus on what they can get. That makes sense, but sometimes the most profound learning comes from what they can give.

In the past, mentoring was conceived as a one-way, one-on-one transaction in which a more knowledgeable individual passed along wisdom, guidance, and insights around a body of knowledge to someone in need of learning. But in our dynamic business environment, many people are challenging that old conception.

Today, the lines between **mentoring** and **networking** are blurring. Welcome to the world of **mentworking**.

Mentworking™ (©Career Systems International) assumes two premises:

▶ Nobody knows it all. As a result, employees should strive to develop the broadest network possible of connections from whom they can learn. The past structure of one mentor to one protégé is history. The new model looks more like a mosaic of connections.

▶ It's reciprocal. Given the diversity in the workplace, there is something to be learned from nearly everyone we encounter. Enlightened mentors can learn as much as they teach.

"My investment in mentoring younger associates is completely selfish. I might have more case experience and a deeper understanding of the law, but that's it. They have entirely new methods for gathering and organizing data that I'm trying to master. They aren't mired in the way-we've-always-done-things-around-here . . . and are always teaching me something new. I get way more than I give in these relationships."

— Attorney/Senior Partner

Teaching is sometimes the best way to learn. Progressive educators have known this for decades. So employees should look not just for people they can learn from, but also those who can learn from them. Lessons in human dynamics, leadership, and communication are just the beginning.

Exposure is all about creating compelling connections among individuals who can share knowledge, skills, and experience. This could be peers, superiors, subordinates, people in other departments, or people outside the organization altogether. And the Internet expands the potential exponentially. You can open the door—and even your contact lists—but the employee has to walk through and take it from there.

EXPERIENCE ENGINEERING

Education and exposure go a long way toward helping employees develop. But experience is frequently the best and most powerful teacher.

Ask any five employees about the most important lessons they've learned and how they learned them. We predict that more than half didn't happen through education, training, or even other people. They happened through the experiences people had. (Read: In many cases, the school of hard knocks.)

WHAT ABOUT YOU?

List the five most significant lessons you've ever learned. Then trace each back to where and when you learned it. How many were a result of education or exposure? If you're like most, the vast majority of your learning has come through experience.

Experience-based learning is the Holy Grail for which many managers have been searching. Most people learn by doing. And there's a lot that needs to be done at work. Strategically bring the two together and you can serve the needs of the organization and individual simultaneously. It's a match made in heaven.

Experience-based learning is about integrating learning into the workflow. Some call it *embedded*; we just call it a sensible way to efficiently and effectively develop others.

"On-the-job learning is my personal favorite . . . in part due to its efficiency. Employees get what they need, and at the same time, we accomplish real work that matters."

— Finance Supervisor

Experience might sound like a big word. But don't be put off by it. Sending employees abroad or starting a new division for someone to head up are certainly experiences. But that's not what we're talking about here.

Experiences can be scaled based upon your **sphere of influence,** the **needs** of the **organization,** and what **employees** are looking to **achieve.**

You have plenty of options—in fact unlimited options—when you consider combinations and permutations of

► Stretch assignments

► Special projects

► Events

► In-department rotations

► Action learning projects and teams

► Job shadowing

► Community service

The most powerful and valuable development experiences involve hands-on, in-the-moment learning. There's no substitute for being confronted by and having to address real business challenges. And, given the number of challenges we face in business, the opportunity to leverage them is limited only by the imagination. Here are some examples.

If the development priority is to . . .	The experience might include . . .
▶ enhance understanding of how customers use the product/service	▶ conducting customer interviews, generating a summary report, and presenting findings at a department meeting
▶ cultivate supervisory and coaching skills	▶ working with all new hires to set expectations, develop job skills, and provide feedback and coaching
▶ broaden exposure to the challenges of delivering services in another territory	▶ standing in for an employee in another office while he/she is on leave

THE ZEN OF EXPERIENTIAL LEARNING

Without getting too deep, there are three truths that a manager must confront before helping people learn through experiences.

▶ With intention and attention, nearly any experience can drive learning and development. The activity doesn't need to be big or flashy. In fact, it can be quite small and insignificant. But learning is possible if employees are focused on making something happen and reflecting on its lessons.

▶ There's no such thing as failure in a learning experience—only failure to learn from it. The quality of the outcome has little to do with the quality of the learning. In fact, according to some experts, humans learn more (and more quickly) through hardships and failure. The key is to wring every bit of insight and learning from the experiences employees have.

▶ Learning is a choice. And it's not yours. Employees must decide to actively engage and learn. You can help them think through how to do it, but they must take responsibility for the hard work of learning.

90%
of all great career-advancing
ideas go

nowhere.

Don't let the ones you help your employees generate suffer that fate. Push those ideas just a little bit farther, enough to make your conversations pay off.

LET'S MAKE A DEAL

Whatever combination of education, exposure, and experience you and your employees arrive at, there needs to be a plan. And the best plans are really development *deals* you strike with employees. Make sure your DEAL is documented, employee owned, aligned with your goals, and linked to the needs of your organization.

Documented — Putting it in writing signals that this is significant and that you are taking it seriously. It acts as a reminder to you and your employees and helps to drive follow-up. Write it on paper or electronically—rather than in concrete. That way you can treat it as the living, breathing, and changeable tool that it is.

Employee owned — If they don't have *buy-in*, you might as well opt out. Employees must take responsibility for their plans and generate the commitment and energy required to implement them. Ownership skyrockets when the plan is personalized to the individual, focused and specific, and doable in light of other activities.

Aligned with the employees' goals — Linking the plan to short-term and long-term goals tests whether activities are worth the effort they will take. When the going gets tough, this overt linkage can sustain focus and energy forward and toward bigger career objectives.

Linked to the needs of the organization — Let's get real here. We all know that resources are in short supply and support can be fickle. Both can be pulled at any time. Don't jeopardize your development efforts. If what employees are doing to learn and develop directly contributes to the bigger picture, you are on safe and solid ground.

SEAL THE DEAL

Development activity is only that—activity—until it is properly un-packed to reveal its lessons. In fact, many employees become so engaged in the experience that they don't take the time to reflect on how they've benefited from it. Yet again, conversation becomes the key to genuine growth. And simple questions help you launch the dialogue.

► What did you learn from that?

► In what ways were you challenged or stretched?

► What pitfalls or obstacles did you discover?

► Why were you successful? Or not?

► What would you do differently?

► What did you discover about yourself in the process?

► What guidelines or principles did you derive?

► How can you use your learning/insight in the future?

► How can you use your learning/insight in other contexts?

► What will you take away from this?

Just one or two of these questions can guide employees toward extracting learning from the experience. In the process you'll seal the deal on their learning and development.

But keep in mind that this sort of debriefing isn't the exclusive domain of the manager. Peers can help unpack learning among themselves. Alternately, skip-level conversations can be powerful, allowing employees to meet, get to know, and gain insights from your manager.

In fact, someone on your team may be looking to develop the ability to help others grow, speak the truth, or challenge others. Wouldn't debriefing another team member's learning be a great experience? Remember, development opportunities are ever-present and limited only by your own imagination.

Powerful possibilities emerge from the hindsight, foresight, and insight conversations you have with employees. But if you identify pos-

> A few minutes of **conversation** can help others slow down enough to reflect, bring deep insights to the surface, **verbalize** important messages, and consider how to **leverage** their expanding skills and knowledge base.

sibilities and insight and then fail to implement them, engagement and job satisfaction are likely to fall lower than if they were never identified at all.

This negative result is completely unnecessary because managers have three powerful ways to translate abstract ideas into tangible action: through education, exposure, and experience.

What IF . . .

► managers and employees were jointly committed to translating the WHAT of career development into doable HOWs?

► employees saw it as their role to help others unpack their learning?

► managers and employees at every level consciously looked for what they could learn from others as well as what they could teach others?

► development activities were considered incomplete until employees had a chance to reflect on and discuss what was learned?

. . . .

9

Grow

with the **FLOW**

For me, it doesn't have to be a big sit-down meeting. In fact, I'd rather it wasn't. Doesn't it seem odd that something as important and personal as someone's career is put on an annual schedule . . . sort of like a termite inspection?

—an employee (perhaps yours)

Want real results? Take career development off the calendar and bring it into real everyday life.

Don't get us wrong. Organizations need individual development planning (IDP) schedules and processes to ensure that career conversations happen. For some employees, it's the only way a development dialogue might ever occur. (Our research indicates that even with those processes in place, nearly 20 percent of those polled still don't get the "annual inspection.")

So, we're all for the regular, planned career conversations—but alone, they just don't cut it.

SUPPLEMENT THE SCHEDULED WITH SPONTANEOUS

What's needed is a more contemporary, organic, and effective way to supplement the scheduled with the spontaneous—to build development into the eternally evolving fabric of the workplace.

Consider the differences between these approaches:

Old Way	vs.	New Way
Taking it all off-line for the annual career discussion (that may be 11 months and 3 weeks away).		Operating real-time: Imagine connecting with employees in the instant, when something has just occurred or has been shared—in that moment of greatest receptivity when emotions (positive or negative) are fresh and people are open to deeper connections and insights.
An artificial scheduled conversation that you and the employee know is mandated by the organization in which you refer to a file of notes that might or might not make sense (since you took them up to 11 months and 3 weeks ago).		An authentic interaction: Imagine a genuine conversation, based upon real and immediate stimulus within the workplace.
A batched approach to addressing career issues, where thirsty people are expected to drink from a fire hose and make it last another year.		An iterative approach: Imagine a layered approach, where information unfolds in digestible chunks, where awareness and insight are built bit by bit over time, where plans are incremental and employees can confidently develop, step by doable step.

Call it what you will: In the moment. On the spot. Context sensitive. Instant. Bite-size. On the fly. Impromptu. Nano-coaching. Stealth development. We call it growing with the flow—workflow, that is.

> **"I learned years ago that career development happens on its own schedule. The annual meeting is nice . . . but I use it more as a chance to summarize and capture highlights. I try to position myself to be there to support others throughout the year when real development—or the chance for it—occurs."**
>
> — Small Business Banker

DROP IN FOR DEVELOPMENT

Growing with the flow means development isn't limited to scheduled meetings and is less burdensome in many ways. It can be quick—as short as one or two minutes. It can be casual—right on the shop floor or hanging over a cubicle wall. It can be completely unplanned—no notes or agendas to contend with. Hardly sounds like work, right?

But in life, there are always tradeoffs. When you grow with the flow, you save time and there is less planning involved. But you've got to be willing to give something as well. And that something in this case is a little more of your attention.

This approach places a new and non-negotiable demand upon managers. It requires that you drop in and heighten your sensitivity to the cues around you. It's as easy—or hard—as that.

Yet, when you think about it, being cue-sensitive is nothing more than a variation on the theme of curiosity.

Cue sensitivity
is curiosity in action.

If you're cultivating curiosity in your conversations, it's not a huge leap to bring curiosity to the world around you. To pick up on what's going on under the surface. To look at situations and events with an eye toward "What can we learn from this?" To see the world around you as fodder for development.

HERE A CUE. THERE A CUE.

Sometimes you can learn more about a concept by studying it from an unusual angle. Along those lines, we've surveyed thousands of individuals across industries and asked them to share examples of times when their managers *missed* important career conversation cues. Which cues from the following list do you think might have come up in our results?

► The employee expresses an interest in learning something new

► Job responsibilities or expectations change

► The employee shares a concern or lack of confidence

► New project launches

► Old project ends

► Uncertain times in the industry or organization

► The employee takes on a new opportunity or assignment

► The employee is passed over for an opportunity or assignment

► New credentials or awards are earned

► The employee inquires about an opportunity

► A high-profile failure occurs

► Low-profile errors are made

► The employee demonstrates extra effort or interest

► Lack of effort or interest is noticed

► The employee shares something interesting he's read, seen, or heard

► Milestones are met

- ▶ Milestones are missed

- ▶ The employee appears to be struggling

- ▶ Things are going poorly

- ▶ Things are going well

Spoiler alert: Don't read farther until you've made your guesses.

We didn't trick you. Real employees—from various roles, levels, and industries—shared every last one of these missed opportunities for development.

WHAT ABOUT YOU?

Review the list again and mark any (it's your book, go ahead, you won't get in trouble) that happened to you over the past week—opportunities for your manager to initiate a career conversation. Then ask yourself which might have occurred with your own employees over the past week. How many of these cues did you follow up on with a conversation?

Cues to grow with the flow abound—whether things are going well or poorly. People are hitting or missing deadlines. Winning or losing. The opportunities to leverage real life for real development are there—if we just develop the habit of looking for them.

POWER OF THE PAUSE

If recognizing a cue is the first step, then what's step two? Cause a pause. Just like tapping the pause button on any electronic device, briefly suspend the action so you can take advantage of the opportunity.

Pausing can redirect the momentum of the moment toward supporting and informing career growth. Here's an example of a possible response from a manager who *doesn't* grow with the flow:

I really lost sleep over that presentation, but it went pretty well.

Employee

Yeah . . . good job!

Manager

This is a nice, reinforcing exchange; but it doesn't drive a career agenda.

YOUR PAUSE PLAYBOOK IN ACTION

The hindsight/foresight/insight framework organizes the career conversations you might have with employees. Each element offers enough breadth and depth (and questions) for one or more very meaty conversations.

But hindsight, foresight, and insight can also work together to create a more comprehensive—yet still brief—conversation that can produce quick but powerful development outcomes. Let's see how that might work on the previous example, with a little play-by-play commentary.

I really lost sleep over that presentation, but it went pretty well.

Employee

A couple of cues present themselves here. The employee feels good about the presentation but also had some concerns. Pause.

I agree. You did a great job. Why'd you lose sleep over it?

Manager

Nice confirmation, but the manager doesn't leave it there. He moves
the ball forward with an opportunity to reflect and look inward and
backward. That's hindsight.

> I've never been all that comfortable presenting
> in front of others. It always makes me nervous.
> Especially with those senior guys in the room.

Employee

> I know. That can be unnerving. What
> did you do that helped make this
> presentation so successful?

Manager

And they're staying in the game with another hindsight question that
helps the employee reflect on strengths, skills, and talents.

> I did my homework and had all the
> right data at my fingertips.

Employee

> Preparation and research are definitely a
> couple of your key strengths. Given the new
> strategic direction, do you see yourself doing
> more or less of this sort of presentation work?

Manager

The manager summarizes the employee's perspective, offering what
could be considered feedback—another bit of hindsight—right before
moving the conversation toward the end zone and connecting it to the
bigger picture with a foresight question.

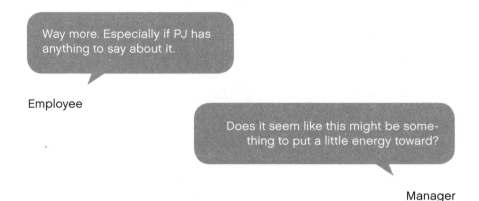

Employee

Manager

With only seconds left on the clock, the manager nimbly weaves together the hindsight and foresight into insight, pointing the employee toward a possibility.

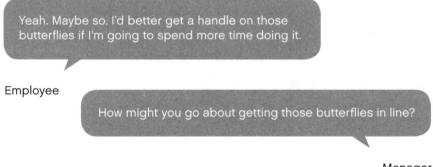

Employee

Manager

But the manager doesn't stop there. He carries the ball across the goal line by moving the conversation into the realm of action. Touchdown!

Growing with the flow by having unplanned conversations like this honors the cadence of business and the authentic, real-time, iterative nature of development. When you spot the cues and cause a pause, you encourage growth not just once a year, but day in and day out.

You're going to have a

conversation

anyway.
Why not take the extra minute to

cause a

pause

and **focus** it toward

career growth?

FOCUSING YOUR FLOW

Growing with the flow is nothing more than a conversation using the questions and approaches sprinkled throughout this book. You have everything you need to seize the moment and turn an opening into a development opportunity.

Pick a question—any question—that lets you delve into hindsight, foresight, or insight.

If the employee is struggling with a project, help look backward at strengths that contributed to the effort and what additional skills might be required. (Hindsight)

" It's counterintuitive, but when things aren't going well, that is the best time to focus on strengths. It gives the employee a needed boost and nearly always surfaces something they can tap into to help the situation. "

— Scientist/Principal Investigator

If the employee shares a story from the news about a competitor, explore what that means for the industry and your own organization. (Foresight)

" It's easy to get sucked into the day-to-day grind. I've got to find every opportunity possible to keep my crew thinking big picture. It helps the hotel and it helps them as individuals. "

— Hospitality Team Leader

If the employee has completed an assignment that was a stretch, open a conversation about the challenges encountered, what was learned, and how it can be applied. (Insight)

" Leaders need to put as much energy in on the back end— debriefing development—as they do setting it up. "

— Executive

Ask any one—a hindsight, foresight, or insight question—and you'll have gone a long way toward seizing the moment and infusing career development into daily life. Ask the three together—and you have an unbeatable combination.

When you make it a habit to grow with the flow, additional benefits follow. Your regularly scheduled career conversations will be richer and more efficient because of the effort you've invested throughout the year. And over time, you'll train employees to pick up on their own cues, cause their own pauses, and take greater ownership for driving their own development. The benefits just keep flowing.

What IF . . .

► employees felt like their careers were precious gems to be polished frequently over time?

► you were in the habit of leveraging day-to-day life at work toward development?

► annual career conversations were the culmination of growing with the flow throughout the year?

CONCLUSION

GROW FOR IT!

Helping employees grow is an essential management responsibility. But for you, it's likely a lot more than that. You didn't go into supervision because you love the scheduling, performance appraisals, and other administrative duties. You did it because of your own career aspirations, your own development, and because you wanted to make a difference in the organization and in those who report to you.

Career development makes a difference.

There are lots of ways to make a difference.

Just talk with people. In today's workplace, everyone knows that employees own their careers. But there's a lot you can do through conversation to help focus, energize, and activate that ownership toward satisfying results by merely talking with employees. **Interact intentionally.**

Keep learning about employees—and help them learn about themselves—throughout their careers. Genuine interest is too frequently in short supply, yet it goes a long way toward building loyalty, retention, and results. Using hindsight as a lens to understand who employees are and what they bring to the party in terms of skills, interests, values, and more will provide a solid foundation for development. **Keep the interview going.**

Encourage and enable foresight. What people are good at, what they love, and how they like to work needs to be filtered through a foresight lens. When you help employees develop the ability to scan the environment, anticipate trends, and spot opportunities, you provide a constructive context for career development. **Foster a future focus.**

Leverage the insights that come from conversations. Help others see where their own hindsight and foresight overlap. Opportunities exist where what employees want to do can find expression in the real, ever-changing world of work. **Mine the intersection of hindsight and foresight for insight.**

Paint a more expansive picture of career development and available growth opportunities. Most people have blinders on when it comes to how to advance their careers. They look only upward. Internalize and promote the climbing wall concept. **Develop in all directions.**

Help others think through how to turn their career goals into action. Ideas and objectives are a good starting point, but they don't get far without the creativity of opportunity mindedness, the tactical focus of planning, and the ongoing conversations that help employees recognize and make the most of education, exposure, and experiences designed for development. **Support the process.**

Find ways to bring development to life day in and day out. Waiting for an annual or pre-scheduled meeting to discuss career matters robs you and your employees of the energy and opportunities that are present always and everywhere. Infuse development conversations into the

CAREER DEVELOPMENT

is one of the most

powerful and underutilized

levers

managers have to **drive**

engagement,

retention,

and

results.

workflow and see how quickly they permeate the culture. **Grow with the flow.**

The reason we all love levers is because their sole purpose is to produce the magic of big results from proportionately smaller forces. If you're wondering where to start, it doesn't matter, because doing something—anything—has significant power.

Start small. Start anywhere.

- ▶ Pick a question and pose it to a single employee.
- ▶ Dedicate the next month to delving into hindsight with one or two employees.
- ▶ Schedule a foresight forum with your group.
- ▶ Share the idea of the career-climbing wall at a team meeting and get reactions.
- ▶ Put the Development Dictionary page from this book in front of an employee and use it to discuss opportunities.
- ▶ Watch for cues to engage in short, spontaneous development discussions.
- ▶ Apply all of this to your next IDP.

What IF . . .

- ▶ **you put just one or two ideas into practice with employees right now?**

· ·

They would grow . . . and so would you.

INDEX

ACKNOWLEDGMENTS

This page cannot begin without expressing our heartfelt appreciation for our collaborator, Ann Jordan.

Ann has worked with Career Systems for 12 years as Vice President of Marketing. To this project, she brought all her smarts, sensibilities, straight talk, and deep savvy about what we could do, should do, and would do! And, in the tight timeframe (that we brought upon ourselves), her conviction and confidence became guiding forces. She kept us buoyed when we needed it, always told us the truth, and jumped for joy when we nailed an idea. She was our first test of a concept, our most helpful critic, and our best audience. We absolutely could not have done this without Ann.

Karen Voloshin also deserves recognition for her early contributions to the book concept. Her creativity, wisdom, and deep appreciation for the audience became part of the fertile soil from which *Help Them Grow or Watch Them Go* grew.

And then there's our publisher, Steve Piersanti. While Bev had worked with Steve for several decades, Julie was new to his uncanny ability to not mince words when he felt we were off track, and to be equally effusive with his praise when we hit the mark. His authenticity, humor, and wisdom were critical to the final product.

Thanks to our design team, Dianne Platner at Berrett-Koehler, Dave Peattie and Tanya Grove at BookMatters, and our artist, Nancy Austin, for catching our vision and enduring the countless *revisions* required to realize it. And our marketing efforts were skillfully guided by Katie

Wacek of Sandia Mountain Marketing and Becky Robinson of Weaving Influence, as well as the Berrett-Koehler team.

The manuscript and all the subsequent steps to produce it were supported by a superb team. We appreciate the continued great work (with oh-so-tight deadlines) from Lindsay Watkins, Lorianne Speaks, Lenore Reggie, and Liz Price. We also appreciate the suggestions and reviews from the Career Systems organization. Everyone read and provided their suggestions and "attagirls" on time and with grace. Thanks particularly to Pat Smith, co-CEO of Career Systems. Pat knew that we had the right team to do this and encouraged us from the very beginning.

The voices of employees and managers throughout *Help Them Grow or Watch Them Go* are the voices we carry around in our minds— the thousands of conversations and interactions with our clients. Their experiences, candor, and wisdom fill each page of this book as they have filled our hearts over the years.

We appreciate our families as well for their many contributions to this effort. Team Giulioni supported Julie from the beginning. Peter, Nick, and Jenna read, critiqued, and celebrated each new step. With Lois Acker's help, they kept the home fires burning during Julie's week-long writing sojourns on Catalina Island. Barry, Lindsey, and Roxy put up with all the working weekends, and Barry accommodated Bev's middle-of-the-night idea scribbling. We certainly could have muddled through without their support; but with it, the process was nothing short of joyful.

And finally, we came to deeply appreciate one another. Introduced years ago by Judy Estrin (thank you!), we had worked together—but never under such tight deadlines or with such expansive goals. This was a true and complete collaboration every single step of the way. We brought different experiences, different styles, different talents, and different backgrounds to the process, and we always marveled at what the other could do. We are both thankful to have had this opportunity and are excited to see where it goes next.

ABOUT THE AUTHORS

PHOTO: MICHAEL NEWAN PHOTOGRAPHY

The authors Julie Winkle Giulioni (left) and Beverly Kaye (right).

BEVERLY KAYE

Dr. Beverly Kaye is an internationally recognized authority on career issues and on retention and engagement in the workplace. She was recently honored with the "Distinguished Contribution" award by the American Society for Training and Development (ASTD) for her groundbreaking and continued impact on workplace learning over the past three decades.

As founder and co-CEO of Career Systems International and a best-selling author on workplace performance, Dr. Kaye and her team have worked with a host of organizations to establish cutting-edge, award-winning talent development solutions. Her first book, *Up Is Not the Only Way,* foresaw the effects that leaner, flatter organizations would have on individual careers and the subsequent need for workers to take charge of their own careers. She also developed learning solutions and systems for managers and employees to work together to help employees achieve their developmental goals.

With the fourth edition of a bestseller she co-authored, *Love 'Em or Lose 'Em: Getting Good People to Stay* (Berrett-Koehler, 2008), Bev addressed one of the most pressing workplace problems of the 21st century: retaining and engaging employees. In her follow-up companion bestseller, *Love It, Don't Leave It: 26 Ways to Get What You Want at Work* (Berrett-Koehler, 2003), she shows employees how they can find greater satisfaction in their current work lives.

Bev is a Jersey Girl but has been living in the LA area for almost 40 years. (Still a Jersey girl!) She's been married for 38 years to her ex–rocket scientist husband, Barry, and is mom to a grown-up daughter, Lindsey, and a grown-up dog, Roxy. She enjoys swimming laps in the summer, skiing in the winter, and breaking bread with friends all year long.

JULIE WINKLE GIULIONI

Julie Winkle Giulioni has spent the past 25 years improving performance through learning. She's partnered with hundreds of organizations to develop and deploy innovative training products that are in use worldwide. Julie is well known and well regarded for her creative, one-of-a-kind solutions that consistently deliver bottom-line results.

As co-founder and principal of DesignArounds, Julie leads multidisciplinary teams that create award-winning electronic and instructor-led training. She is an author and respected speaker on a variety of topics, including performance improvement, leadership, sales, and customer service.

Previously Julie was the director of product development for AchieveGlobal, one of the world's largest commercial training and development companies. She has also held training management positions in financial services and retail organizations, taught marketing at the secondary and post-secondary level, and served as a department chair at Woodbury University.

When Julie is not working with clients, she's an active community member and PTA/soccer mom. A Southern California native, she's as comfortable doing stand-up paddle boarding as she is doing stand-up training. Julie currently lives with her husband, Peter, their two children, Jenna and Nick, and a puppy, Pixel, in South Pasadena.

WORKING WITH THE AUTHORS

Bev and Julie each have their own independent companies that offer an array of specialized products and services. They came together to create this powerful book on developing talent through career conversations, and they partner often in their separate consulting practices. Both deliver exceptional keynote speeches globally and have their own websites in addition to Help-Them-Grow.com.

CAREER SYSTEMS INTERNATIONAL
A Beverly Kaye Company

Beverly Kaye founded Career Systems International (CSI) more than three decades ago to offer innovative ways to help organizations solve their greatest talent challenges by engaging, developing, and retaining their people.

CSI provides a comprehensive portfolio of award-winning learning solutions and services globally to a broad base of industries and organizations including nearly two-thirds of the Fortune 1000 companies. Our delivery team is a deeply experienced cadre of consul-

Our unique approach to organizational learning has always demanded solutions that are deceptively simple, delightfully engaging, deliberately flexible, and decidedly business centric. These principles always guide us in developing and delivering solutions that provide high impact and measurable results.

tants and facilitators with a parallel capacity to bring our solutions to internal practitioners as well. Our customer service and client success teams ensure all client engagements exceed customer expectations.

Conversations are the common thread and outcome for all of our areas of expertise. Simple, but powerful, these critical conversations around engaging, growing, mentoring, and retaining talent ignite vital connections between employees, managers, and their organizations. Clients consistently report that they get powerful results as they create a strong voice for all their people in a surround-sound world.

Our mission is to improve the business performance of our clients and the lives of all employees who seek to maximize their personal and professional potential. We do this by providing the best employee engagement, career development, and retention solutions on the planet.

HOW WE CAN PARTNER WITH YOU

Career Development: Career development consistently ranks as a top driver in employee engagement, not only impacting retention but also fueling an organization with innovative, productive, and impassioned employees. CSI's CareerPower suite teaches employees to self-power their careers and teaches managers to act as sounding board and career coach to drive the learning and growth of the individuals on their team. These solutions are highly interactive with assessments, tools, and activities to have managers and employees return to the job with actionable plans, the skill, and the confidence to hold meaningful development conversations and create a culture where learning and growth is ongoing and organizational talent is optimized to meet company goals.

Engaging and Retaining Talent: Engaging people and impacting business results requires managers to have a unique set of skills to effectively influence employee commitment. Love 'Em or Lose 'Em: Getting Good People to Stay, CSI's solution based on the *Wall Street Journal*'s bestseller co-authored by Bev Kaye, provides today's leaders with the experience, knowledge, communication, and confidence to drive impassioned employment worldwide. Though managers play a crucial role, employees can also take charge of their own satisfaction. SatisfACTION Power is CSI's employee learning experience, based on Bev's bestseller *Love It, Don't Leave It*, which empowers individuals to create the conditions they need to improve job satisfaction without having to leave. As managers hold "Stay Interviews" and employees become comfortable in their roles, engagement truly becomes a two-way street, and business results are maximized.

Mentoring the Multitudes: Today mentors are found at all levels in an organization, and people at all levels have wisdom to share with others, despite organization titles. Imagine a workplace where mentoring is prominent, mentors are mentoring many, and individuals are seeking multiple mentors. People would constantly be learning and find excitement in their work. CSI's **PowerMentoring** solutions provide a framework for both mentors and learning partners to get the most out of their relationships. Mentoring—and the ensuing conversations—are powerful and cost-effective ways to impact talent.

Consulting Support: Our consultant team understands the importance of providing a strategic perspective to maximize business results for all of our solutions. We work to focus on an organization's culture, resource requirements, human resource structures, long-range goals, and business plans. The more our learning solutions are embedded in the larger system, the more impactful they can be.

CareerSystemsIntl.com or 1-800-577-6916

DESIGNAROUNDS

Julie Winkle Giulioni and her partner, Karen Voloshin, are co-founders and principals of DesignArounds, a bi-coastal consulting, training, and development firm, committed to maximizing individual and organizational potential.

DesignArounds develops enterprise-wide learning experiences to help employees master new skills and apply them to key business objectives. We create streamlined training designs built on the latest research into how adults learn and produce innovative and appealing materials in print, video, and electronic formats. Additionally, we can help you

► Tie learning experiences to critical strategic business initiatives through technology-enabled, classroom, and blended solutions

► Ensure results by extending learning beyond the classroom through assessments, coaching, and on-the-job application

► Re-energize and update your existing training with the most current and effective methods and learning activities

With DesignArounds, you can always count on learning that's absolutely relevant; engaging, challenging, and fun; meaningfully interactive; rich with choices, practical tools, and strategies; and focused on results

► Make training sticky through stakeholder buy-in, reinforcement, and evaluation strategies

► Provide coaching to support people in applying what they have learned and to improve personal effectiveness

DESIGNAROUNDS:
Designed around you!

Julie Winkle Giulioni & Karen Voloshin
626-799-3418 | www.designarounds.com | 203-393-2261

By Beverly Kaye and Sharon Jordan-Evans

Love 'Em or Lose 'Em
Getting Good People to Stay, 4th Edition

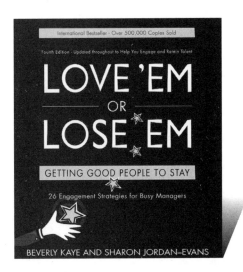

Talent is everything. That's why engagement and retention matter more than ever before. Every employee who walks out the door costs the company up to 200 percent of his or her annual salary to replace, and survey after survey reports that employees are unhappy and not working up to their full potential. As a manager, you need your best people to stay with you longer, fully engaged and producing at their peak. The latest edition of this *Wall Street Journal* bestseller offers twenty-six simple strategies—from A to Z—that managers can use to address their employees' real concerns and keep them engaged. Good economy or bad, your best people always have choices. Will they choose you? You have the power to make a difference. *Love 'Em or Lose 'Em* shows you what to do.

Paperback, 306 pages, ISBN 978-1-57675-557-0
PDF ebook, ISBN 978-1-57675-776-5

Berrett–Koehler Publishers, Inc.
www.bkconnection.com

800.929.2929

Love It, Don't Leave It

26 Ways to Get What You Want at Work

Whether for fear of an uncertain economy or reluctance to deal with the inevitable stresses of looking for work, many people feel unwilling or unable to change jobs. So they simply "quit on the job." They disengage, produce less, and bide their time in quiet dissatisfaction. This *Wall Street Journal* bestseller provides readers with twenty-six ways to make their current work environment more satisfying. Presented in an appealing, accessible A-to-Z format, *Love It, Don't Leave It* includes strategies for improving communication, stimulating career growth, balancing work with family, and much more. Designed for workers at any age and at any stage, *Love It, Don't Leave It* helps people assume responsibility for the way their work lives work.

Paperback, 225 pages, ISBN 978-1-57675-250-0
PDF ebook, ISBN 978-1-57675-875-5

Berrett–Koehler Publishers, Inc.
www.bkconnection.com

800.929.2929

❇ Berrett–Koehler
B̄K̄ Publishers

Berrett-Koehler is an independent publisher dedicated to an ambitious mission: *Creating a World That Works for All*.

We believe that to truly create a better world, action is needed at all levels—individual, organizational, and societal. At the individual level, our publications help people align their lives with their values and with their aspirations for a better world. At the organizational level, our publications promote progressive leadership and management practices, socially responsible approaches to business, and humane and effective organizations. At the societal level, our publications advance social and economic justice, shared prosperity, sustainability, and new solutions to national and global issues.

A major theme of our publications is "Opening Up New Space." Berrett-Koehler titles challenge conventional thinking, introduce new ideas, and foster positive change. Their common quest is changing the underlying beliefs, mindsets, institutions, and structures that keep generating the same cycles of problems, no matter who our leaders are or what improvement programs we adopt.

We strive to practice what we preach—to operate our publishing company in line with the ideas in our books. At the core of our approach is stewardship, which we define as a deep sense of responsibility to administer the company for the benefit of all of our "stakeholder" groups: authors, customers, employees, investors, service providers, and the communities and environment around us.

We are grateful to the thousands of readers, authors, and other friends of the company who consider themselves to be part of the "BK Community." We hope that you, too, will join us in our mission.

A BK Business Book

This book is part of our BK Business series. BK Business titles pioneer new and progressive leadership and management practices in all types of public, private, and nonprofit organizations. They promote socially responsible approaches to business, innovative organizational change methods, and more humane and effective organizations.

Berrett–Koehler
Publishers

A community dedicated to creating
a world that works for all

Visit Our Website: www.bkconnection.com

Read book excerpts, see author videos and Internet movies, read our
authors' blogs, join discussion groups, download book apps, find out about
the BK Affiliate Network, browse subject-area libraries of books, get special
discounts, and more!

Subscribe to Our Free E-Newsletter, the *BK Communiqué*

Be the first to hear about new publications, special discount offers, exclusive articles, news about bestsellers, and more! Get on the list for our free
e-newsletter by going to **www.bkconnection.com**.

Get Quantity Discounts

Berrett-Koehler books are available at quantity discounts for orders of ten or
more copies. Please call us toll-free at (800) 929-2929 or email us at **bkp
.orders@aidcvt.com**.

Join the BK Community

BKcommunity.com is a virtual meeting place where people from around
the world can engage with kindred spirits to create a world that works for
all. BKcommunity.com members may create their own profiles, blog, start
and participate in forums and discussion groups, post photos and videos,
answer surveys, announce and register for upcoming events, and chat with
others online in real time. Please join the conversation!

MIX
From responsible
sources
FSC® C113845
FSC
www.fsc.org

Certified
Corporation
bcorporation.net